CHARL ... TIN

FLOOD

GLOBAL CLUES OF A COMMON EVENT

LEGENDS

First printing: May 2009

Master Books®, P.O. Box 726, Green Forest, AR 72638.

ISBN-13: 978-0-89051-553-2
ISBN-10: 0-89051-553-0
Library of Congress Number: 2009923590

Unless otherwise noted, all Scripture is from the New International Version of the Bible.

Printed in the United States of America

Please visit our website for other great titles:
www.masterbooks.net

For information regarding author interviews, please contact the publicity department at (870) 438-5288.

Master
Books®
A Division of New Leaf Publishing Group
www.masterbooks.net

*To my mom, who, no doubt, has already
asked Him where the vessel landed.
You'll have to tell me when I get there, Mom.*

Acknowledgments

How can I even begin to sum up a lifetime of inspirations in just a few short paragraphs? This isn't easy, so if I have forgotten to mention you by name, I'm sorry; I hope you can forgive the slight.

First, I want to thank my loving wife, Virginia. What could I possibly say to make up for all those evenings you spent alone while I feverishly worked on draft after draft? Thank you for your patience and support. I love you.

And I'd like to thank our cats for *not* eating the pages we had strewn across the house for the better part of a month.

Thanks, also, to my father, Charles, for always encouraging me to follow my passions. This ranks pretty high on the list of things I'm excited about.

I owe an enormous thank-you to the "Young Professionals" class at Bethany Place. You guys have spent the last five years challenging me to always dig deeper into the Word. Thanks.

And where would this book be if it weren't for the intellectual giants who have come before, and on whose shoulders I have merely stood? I am indebted to the work of the late Sir James Frazer and Theodore Gaster. Their collection of world mythology is unprecedented. I am also deeply indebted to the work and studies of the Institute for Creation Research and the Answers in Genesis organization.

Thank you to Tim Dudley, Laura Welch, and the rest of the staff at New Leaf for believing in an unpublished author with an unpolished manuscript. I — literally — could not have done this without you. Thank you.

Lastly, thank You to my Lord and Savior, Jesus Christ. Despite my doubts and disobedience, He still *likes* me, and even calls me "friend." For that, I am eternally perplexed . . . but thankful, nonetheless.

CONTENTS

Chapter 1

MYTH: HISTORY OR LEGEND?

Bid me discourse, I will enchant thine ear.[1]
— William Shakespeare

*M*ythology. The very word conjures up different images for different people. Some picture the gods and goddesses of ancient Rome: Jupiter, Mercury, and the bloodthirsty war-god, Mars. Some picture the Minotaur of Greek mythology, hiding deep in his labyrinth lair, waiting to devour his next victim. Others may picture the slightly more obscure animal spirits of Native American legends, or the tree-spirits of Celtic lore. Regardless of what we may picture, nearly everyone, in some way, is drawn to mythology.

With the popularity of movies such as *Jason and the Argonauts*, *Ben-Hur*, *Troy*, *King Arthur*, *Alexander*, *300*, even

Finding Neverland, film companies and moviegoers have long attempted to discern the difference between reality and fiction. We all seem to have the desire to find — are perhaps even obsessed with finding — the fine line that often exists between history and legend. What is it that draws us to mythology? What makes ancient folklore so irrevocably attractive to us? Do we simply love a good yarn? Are we drawn to it for the entertainment, or do we sometimes feel the tug of a memory — a feeling that our history is, somehow, embedded in the stories?

In the past, mythologists have approached ancient literature with a certain amount of skepticism: myths, they felt, were nothing more than fanciful literature — imaginative inventions of creative minds — and therefore could not, and *should* not, be taken as literal history. But is this true? Is a myth nothing more than a child's bedtime story, a fable to be outgrown? Not every mythologist feels that way, however. The last century has seen a shift in how we regard mythology. Since the late 1800s, mythologists have come to see myth as not *wholly* fictional, but instead as *embellishments* of truth. In other words, a "complex" myth may, in fact, have a perfectly "reasonable" footing in "reality."

There are two basic basic approaches to interpreting myths. The first approach is one of utter disregard for the tales, legends, and recorded history of a group of people. The second approach is an attempt to "symbolize" the stories by discounting the telling of them as distorted and exaggerated versions of the truth. What mythologists who take this approach believe is that the mythical event happened, but not necessarily as it was told. The events, they argue, may have been "real," but the interpretation — the version passed down — has been exaggerated and distorted well beyond the "true" event. A perfect example of a myth that suffers from both of these interpretive styles, and one we will be looking at in more detail later, is that of the global Flood.

The story of the Flood permeates nearly every culture of the world in some way, shape, or form. While some of the details vary between the different cultural versions, the same basic plotline occurs in all of them: a god becomes angry and destroys the earth with a flood but preserves the human race by selecting a certain number of people to survive the catastrophe. These people are saved from the flood by a vessel, which carries them throughout the duration of the event. In the stories, it is this same group of people that is then responsible for repopulating the earth.

Despite these striking similarities, some mythologists have looked at the *differences* in the various versions and declared: "This never happened!" The differences, they often claim, are too great, and the premise is too far-fetched. They may look at the fact that Noah builds an ark, while a group of aborigines in Australia build a raft and claim that the differences make the story impossible.

On the other hand, many claim that a flood did indeed occur, but that it was a "local" flood and its occurrence was merely misunderstood and overstated. "Noah's flood" and the "Aborigine flood" were not so much global catastrophes as they were local disasters. I feel both of these interpretive styles stem from an unfortunate mindset: the belief that we know better than the people who came before us.

We believe we live in an age of "progressive" thinking. Personally, I prefer to call it "contradictory" thinking. We contradict ourselves in that, while we wish to be open-minded and rational, we stop using our minds if stories seem too "illogical"; we dismiss them outright as fairy tales. In other words, we close our minds just when we should be opening them more, and in the process disregard what may, in fact, be truth. This is not to say that ancient cultures were more technologically advanced than we are today — after all, they did not have computers, cars, or electricity — but it is not fair to say that they were less *intelligent*. Does owning a car translate into having a better grasp on "reality"? Does having a computer mean that we understand events of the past better than the people who may have experienced them? Two extremely cogent examples of this thinking spring immediately to mind. The first involves the myth of Troy and a blind bard's tale of war and betrayal. The second example involves the myth of the Kraken.

Of Wars and Cephalopods

Prior to 1870, most scholars regarded Homer's *Iliad* as pure fiction. However, in the early 1870s two archaeologists, Heinrich Schliemann and Frank Calvert, excavated several artifacts in the Turkish desert, including a city that had been burned to the ground just as Homer had reported. Even more importantly, however, they uncovered within the ruins a coin engraved "Ilium," the ancient Latin name for Troy (and the source for the title of Homer's *Iliad*). Sadly, while historians did *eventually* begin to take a more serious look at Homer's work, it took until the late 19th century for the battle of the *Iliad* to even be acknowledged as *possible*. In essence then, Troy had been destroyed twice prior to the excavations — first in battle, and then in the minds of the educated. Today, we still do likewise. We believe that if a story or historical account does not mesh with practical sensibilities, we cannot accept it, and we want everything to be proven before we will believe it. I've found, however, that lack of *proof* does not necessarily mean lack of *truth*. Another example of this idea, made popular in recent movies, is the myth of the Kraken.

The Kraken appears most notably in Norse and Icelandic mythology, but its stories were also popular with American whalers, who brought many of the legends with them from the Old World. This is not to say, however, that the whalers were responsible for *every* tale of the Kraken on this side of the Atlantic, because similar tales already existed here. In Peru, for example, Native American fishermen would tell tales of a water demon that closely resembled the Kraken of Norse mythology.[2]

The beast was said to be a form of cephalopod, like the common octopus or squid. Descriptions of its size varied, but it was reported to have tentacles long enough to drag a ship under the waves. In the middle of the 1700s, Bishop Pontoppidan, a well-known but often criticized biologist (or "naturalist," as they were then called), described, at length, the Scandinavian Kraken. He wrote that it "looks at first like a number of small islands, surrounded with something that floats and fluctuates like sea weeds." He then described that, as one nears it, the "sea weeds" look more like "horns [i.e., arms] . . . which grow thicker and thicker the higher they rise above the surface of the water." He finishes by asserting that the "horns," when jutting straight up out of the ocean, "stand as high and large as the masts of middle-siz'd vessels."[3] Pliny the Elder discusses the Kraken at length in his *Naturalis Historia*, written sometime in the first century A.D. Pliny actually calls the creature a "polyp," but his description matches that given of the Kraken in other literature. He describes it as a fierce beast with a jelly-like body, long tentacles, and a sharp, parrot-like beak.

Despite the numerous tales, though, naturalists for several centuries dismissed the Kraken as an imaginary creature. A sighting, they seemed to argue, had never been "confirmed," and therefore the beast could not possibly be real. Elsewhere in the world, tales of other giant cephalopods were told, but these were dismissed, as well. Even in 1861, when a French crew on the *Allecton* actually *harpooned* a giant squid, or *Architeuthis*, managing to save the tail section, tales of the Kraken were still soundly ignored by naturalists.[4] It was not until a full specimen of a giant squid washed up on the shore of New-foundland 12 years later that giant cephalopods were finally taken seriously by the scientific community.

From that point on, specimens of the giant squid — always dead and badly decomposing when they washed ashore — were studied intently. It became the general belief that they could achieve lengths of up to 60 feet. The first living giant squid to be photographed was in 2004, when a team of Japanese researchers at the Ogasawara Whale Watching Association managed to catch sight of one in the waters off the coast of Japan. In 2006, that same group was able to vid-eotape, for the first time, a living giant squid.[5] Incidentally, the squid was "only" 24 feet long, and considered a juvenile. Whether or not the giant squid is the precise creature that the Norwegian fishermen had in mind when they told each other tales of the Kraken is of little relevance. The point is that giant cephalopods — and therefore the Kraken — *do* exist. However, despite the earlier tales, the Kraken as an actual living creature was blatantly disregarded by scientists until the latter part of the 19th century.

Once more, this is the first approach to mythology: utter disbelief. The mantra seems to be, "If we don't believe it, then it *can't* be true." I wonder, though, how much of our history — and *natural* history — is being disregarded each time we take this stance. What insights into ancient Greece might we have gained by now if we had taken Homer's poem seriously? Would biological research into giant cephalopods be further along if we had begun it, say, in 1773, instead of 1873? Some mythologists, realizing this, have taken a different approach to their study. This approach is to accept some myths as not *simply* fact, but as *embellished* fact. In other words, the myths are partially true, but not entirely accurate.

We see this, once again, in the story of the Deluge. Because so many cultures speak of a flood, it is argued, they each must have experienced some form of flooding. The prevailing theory is that, because cultures settle near water, each would have experienced the destructive force of a "local flood" at some point. In my own town, on the banks of the James River, we experience severe flash flooding whenever a hurricane comes through the area; local floods are a necessary evil when living near water. A relatively new book, published in 1998, even suggests that the Genesis account was based on the flooding of the Black Sea, sometime at the end of the last Ice Age.[6]

This interpretation — that the myths are based on localized flooding — is exceptionally convenient, because it accounts for all of the differences that we find between Native American, Greek, Hebrew, Indian, and other versions of the myth.[7] After all, if each culture developed the story based on local events, then we would *expect* variation between the different cultural versions. However, what it fails to account for are the striking *similarities* among the different versions, several of which we will address in later chapters. If separate cultures invented separate stories, of course they would differ. But if separate cultures developed separate stories, why would they be identical in some aspects? The "independent evolution" stance cannot account for that.

Not only does the "independent evolution" theory fail to account for the similarities among the stories, it also severely undermines the intelligence of these cultures. Surely cultures intelligent enough to build ocean-going vessels know the difference between river valley floods and a global flood. Few would question the intelligence of the advanced Hindu culture that produced the *Mahābhārata* and *Ramayana*, and yet many scholars attribute its flood story (*Mahābhārata*, Book III) to the cyclic flooding of the Ganges River. On the same token, do we believe that the Greeks, whose governmental, philosophical, and artistic ideas still influence us today, truly mistook a local flood for a global deluge, as is reported in their story of Deucalion and Pyrrah? Does it really seem sensible that such intelligent cultures would make such simple oversights? It does not seem likely at all.

There is, therefore, one other alternative, and that is to accept that the different versions all refer to the *same event*. In other words, what if we accept that there was a group of people that survived a global deluge, and that the story of the event was passed on from generation to generation through various developing cultures? What would that look like? We would expect to see two things. First, we would expect to see similar, if not identical, plots spread throughout the various versions. At the same time, we would expect to see diverging details — perhaps even *contradictory* details — as the story spread. I call this process — the process of one story being told many different ways as it progresses through time — telephone mythology.

Telephone

Most of us have played the game. A dozen people sit in a circle, and one person whispers a phrase to the person next to him or her. That person then whispers the phrase to a third person, who, in turn, whispers to the next, and so on. When the very last person has "received" the message, he or she speaks it aloud, only to discover — usually to the delight of everyone — that it has been changed and distorted. History is really no different.

Anthropology more or less *requires* one of two views when analyzing the development of cultures. The first view requires the separate major cultures found throughout the world to have evolved in their homelands, independent of each other, in an amoeba-to-man process. Each culture, as it developed, would create its own set of mythologies for such things as the elements, sickness, and so forth. One such myth that each culture would have developed would have been a story of a deluge, sent by an angry deity to wipe out life on earth. Those who survive do so because of a miraculous intervention in their lives by a creator god who provides them with either the instructions for building a vessel, or the vessel itself. What we often find is that this deluge story is followed by a story of a diaspora, or a spreading of cultures from a central point. According to some, the flood portion of the tale is inspired by something like the annual flooding of a local river. The diaspora portion, then, would be nothing more than an attempt on the part of the storytellers to describe the origins of other existing cultures with which they may have come into contact from time to time. This view is commonly held among mythologists, anthropologists, and the scientific and literary community as "accurate."

The second — and less common view — requires an *actual* deluge, followed by an *actual* diaspora, which *results* in separately evolving cultures, each of which carries a part of the story with it. When the vessel of the deluge lands and the families begin to disperse and develop their own cultures, they each hold onto the details that pertain to their own evolving belief systems. As time passes and those cultures begin to fragment into other cultures, we would expect to see other changes in the story; this is only natural. In fact, we would expect that the further from the source (both temporal and physical) the story moves, the more it would change. However, even more curiously, when we then add thousands of years, countless people, and a scattering of these people, we find that, despite changes, there are *still common threads*. The first view — the "local flood" or "independent evolution" view — can reasonably explain the differences in the versions. It cannot, however, explain all of the similarities. Indeed, how can we account for these common threads, unless we admit that the stories all originate from the same source?

The telephone mythology view is the only view that explains both the similarities and the differences.

This is in no way an attempt to undermine the other mythological disciplines, for they each have their place. While we need not believe that Apollo sails across the sky in his chariot, is it distasteful to believe in someone with the characteristics of Hercules? Should we fictionalize Samson? This is simply presenting *another* way to look at myth. So what are we to do? Are we to blindly accept every story we hear as children? Should we believe that a pernicious little rabbit hopped about in a blue coat, stealing vegetables from a certain farmer's garden? Should we rewrite history books to include, as fact, every novel published? Do we admit that H.G. Wells' *Time Machine* really happened?

No, of course not! Yet to immediately dismiss mythology outright, or to oversimplify mythology in an attempt to make it more palatable to our modern way of thinking, is intellectually irresponsible because it *potentially dismisses our very own history*. We once disregarded the *Iliad* simply because we *chose* to disregard it. We once dismissed tales of the Kraken simply because we *chose* to dismiss them. Just because we *regard* certain things as fictional does not give us the right to immediately *dismiss* them as fictional.

Yet if we are to discuss whether or not to dismiss mythology, we have to decide whether or not a myth is reasonable. After all, we cannot — in a very practical sense — examine *every* myth for historical accuracy, for there are far too many, and several of them contradict each other. Where, then, do we start in this process? What criteria do we use to determine the "reasonability" of a myth? How do we know if a myth is historical, without actually having been there to witness the events?

Furthermore, how do we even *define* myth? Is "myth" one broad category in literature or is there more than one kind of "myth"? Is myth always fictional, or *can* it be historical, as well? The next chapter looks at some of these questions.

Endnotes

1. William Shakespeare, *Venus and Adonis*. Line 145.
2. Michael Bright, *There Are Giants in the Sea* (London: Robson Books Ltd., 1989), p. 156 .
3. E. Pontoppidan, *The Natural History of Norway*, 1775. Quoted by Richard Ellis, *Monsters of the Sea* (New York: Alfred A. Knopf, 1994), p. 125.
4. Ibid, p. 121.
5. "Japanese Researchers Capture Giant Squid," Fox News, December 22, 2006.
6. William Ryan and Walter Pitman, *Noah's Flood: The New Scientific Discoveries About the Event That Changed History* (New York: Simon & Schuster, 1998).
7. See appendix B for several versions of the Flood story.

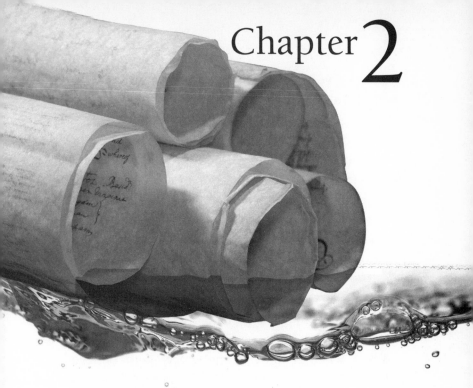

Chapter 2

WHAT *IS* MYTH?

Hearken! And I shall tell you the whole tale.
— Edgar Allen Poe, "The Tell-Tale Heart"

Our word "myth" comes from the Greek word *mythos*, meaning "story, speech, or legend." To the Greeks, a *mythos* "may" have been fictional, but it may also have been true. I could, for example, tell you the myth of Santa, his toy-making elves, and his eight flying reindeer. On the other hand, I could tell you the wholly truthful myth of my trip to the market yesterday morning. This basic definition of myth — that "myth" is simply a story, which may or may not be true — is the definition we will be using throughout this book. Whenever I refer to "myth," therefore, I am not necessarily commenting on the *historical value* of the myth, but am simply using the word interchangeably with "story."

If, in the scope of this study, "myth" can be either true or false, how do we initially assess the accuracy of a myth? After all, without being there to witness the events described, can we *truly* tell if a myth is accurate? Honestly, no . . . not with any guarantee, at least. So how do we do this? If we cannot assume *everything* written is false, but neither can we *guarantee validity* without witnessing the event, then what approach do we take when studying mythology? Can we continue to study it, or are we at an impasse? There are, I believe, two aspects that we need to evaluate before determining whether or not a myth is worth pursuing as history.

Many prefer to pursue the validity of a myth by first assessing whether or not the storytellers believed the myth to be true. This is the first aspect. William Bascom, professor of anthropology at the University of California, Berkeley, breaks down "myth" into three categories: myth, folklore, and legend. Myth, he argues, is regarded as fact by the culture, while folklore is regarded as fiction, even by the storytellers. Legend is regarded as true, he asserts, but the events of the legend are not quite as distant as the events of a myth.[1] What does this all mean? What I believe he is arguing is that the real key lies in determining the *motivation* behind the storytellers. If we are to pursue myth as history, we must determine whether or not the cultures themselves believed the stories to be true.

This is a good place to start. Whether or not a culture regards a myth as history should be the first sign for which we look: if it was history for them, perhaps it should be history for us as well. While this is an excellent start, however — and I want to emphasize this — it is only a *start*. There is a second aspect that I feel we should take into consideration when determining whether to pursue a myth as history. This second aspect involves looking at whether the myth is a myth of *nature*, or a myth of *event*.

Myths of Nature vs. Myths of Event

For most cultural literature, myth falls into one of these two categories. What is the difference? A myth from either of these categories *may* contain the intervention of a deity, the myth *may* contain a moral lesson to be learned, and it *may* involve humans. The main difference between the two categories is found in the *primary purpose* of the myth. Does the myth serve, primarily, to narrate an *event*, or does it serve to explain *nature*? The story of Narcissus transforming into a flower is far different from the story and witness of Christ. One attempts to explain the origin of a flower, the other bears the story of our Savior's life and death. One explains, the other narrates. One is a myth of nature, the other a myth of event.

Myths of event unfold a narrative that tells of the intervention of gods in the world of men. They may, as well, tell of superhuman feats achieved by human characters. Sometimes there is a moral, sometimes not, but they *always exist, first and foremost, to tell a "story."* The *Iliad* is an example of such a myth. A ten-year war fought with the aid of the gods and goddesses of Greek culture contains the necessary elements for the event myth: a story regarded as history (and now known to be at least partially true), but with an element of the supernatural. While there are morals and lessons to be learned throughout the narrative, the poem itself is written with an authority that treats it more as a history lesson than a fable. To all appearances, it was regarded as an actual war by the Greeks. What is more important, however, is that the war *was* an actual war, and Troy an actual city.

Myths of nature show distinct tendencies to be explanatory — to describe a phenomenon in the world that was inexplicable with the science of the time. One such myth, the myth of Apollo's chariot, tells of the god Phoebus Apollo, who sails across the heavens in his chariot of fire each day.[2] The myth clearly attempts to explain the path of the sun through the sky. While it is an interesting and fascinating story, we know it to be scientifically incorrect because the mechanism behind the process can be explained. Technology has given us the ability to observe the earth in space and to see the sun for what it is . . . and what it is *not*. It *is*, for example, a furnace of nuclear energy. It is *not* a shining god in a golden chariot, racing through the heavens.

Likewise, we know that lightning forms at neither the hand of the Roman god Jupiter, nor at the hand of the Hindu god Indra. Myths of nature may serve to explain the mysterious world around its tellers, but the cultures that designed such myths did not have the convenience of weather balloons, probes, or a working knowledge of electricity. As such, they were forced to devise an explanation that could be plausibly accepted. For them, the gods who aid in battle and boost the fertility of crops are the same beings who send lightning from the sky. This does not mean that they were less intelligent than we are today; it simply means that the tools for understanding nature were not available. While myths of nature *are* narratives by necessity, they do not serve to narrate the history of a culture, but serve, instead, to explain a *natural* phenomenon. Incidentally, what many people — mythologists included — seem to forget is that myths of nature are not restricted to the past. Modern myths of nature abound today. One example is that of the big-bang theory.

Having rejected the creation myths of cultures around the world, astronomers sought to find the origin of the universe. In 1929, Edwin Hubble observed that the universe appeared to be expanding, and cosmologists searched for an explanation. The theory they developed was that of an event now called the big bang.

We would call the big bang a *living* myth because it is still evolving and growing. Like the earlier creation myths that preceded it, it changes and grows as discoveries are made and the scientific culture changes. In other words, the myth morphs into an "acceptable" form with each new discovery.[3] Neither this constant change, nor the initial rejection of other creation myths, diminishes the reality that the universe has a beginning; the story of its beginning simply changes to suit the teller. It seems that modern cosmology, you see, has simply replaced older myths with a newer myth.

Myths of nature explain the world around us, sometimes correctly, sometimes incorrectly. Myths of nature give comfort to us because — until new myths emerge to replace the old ones — they provide meaning to a chaotic natural environment. Myths of nature are also generally easy to either prove or disprove, and therefore are not extremely useful to study through the lens of telephone mythology. We may pursue them through other avenues like astronomy, physics, and biology, of course, but from a literary and historical standpoint, myths of nature hold little interest for us. There are always exceptions, and as such, the two are not always mutually exclusive. One could argue, for example, that many of the creation myths are both a type of event myth *and* a type of nature myth. However, in our study of telephone mythology, myths of nature are not really brought into the equation.

On the other hand, myths of event explain *who we are*, as both members of humanity and as members of a distinct culture. They detail significant events in the lives of people, events that often changed the course of history. Because none of us were there when the event myths happened, many of them are difficult to either prove or disprove. Unless we can find *irrefutable* evidence that an event never occurred, therefore, event myths should seldom be taken for granted. Does this mean we accept all event myths as accurate? No, because we must always weigh the evidence. And what if the evidence is unclear? Telephone mythology, as a means of studying event myths, will help us in those cases. This brings us back to the Deluge Myth.

The Deluge requires us to look at the development of cultures from around the world, and the way their beliefs — expressed in their mythology — are presented. Once again, however, we look not only at how this myth shapes our perception of the cultures we study, but how those *individual cultures* influence the telling of the myth; we must examine how the myth *changes* with the culture that is telling it.

Like the beginning of the universe, the reality of a global flood is in no way diminished by the various retellings of the story. Just as innumerable creation myths tell us that there *must* have been a beginning, in whatever form, the flood myths around the world tell us that there *must* have been a Flood. Likewise, however, just as the earlier nature myths have been rejected, so have the earlier event myths. We must then ask a very serious question: how can we be sure that our new myths are more accurate?

Perhaps they are not. Perhaps in discarding many of the old myths, we have discarded truth. Perhaps we have discarded our very history. Perhaps we have replaced that history with a false myth, a false myth that, though it seems more "probable" to our minds today, is simply wrong. Instead of global flood myths, we reinterpret them as local flood myths. The question, though, remains: can we *reasonably* do that? I believe a serious look at literature is necessary at this point in our development. So let's approach mythology with an open mind; let's *pursue* truth rather than *assume* it. Let's see if the literature lends itself credibility instead of taking it, without hesitation, as false.

We'll start by looking at just a few of the diaspora myths, and see how telephone mythology applies. We'll look briefly at why I believe telephone mythology is a very viable form of study. Then we'll turn to our global flood myth and see if, perhaps, telephone mythology can help us lend credibility to the different flood legends.

Endnotes
1. William Bascom, "The Forms of Folklore: Prose Narrative," in *Sacred Narrative*, Alan Dundes, editor (Berkely, CA: University of California Press, 1984), p. 11.
2. See appendix C for a portion of the text.
3. Marcus Chown, "Before the Big Bang," *New Scientist* (June 3, 2000): no. 2241.

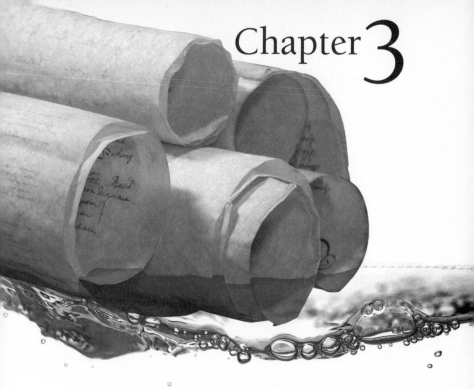

Chapter 3

THE DIASPORA

> *So the LORD scattered them from there over all the earth; and they stopped building the city. That is why it was called Babel — because there the LORD confused the language of the whole world. From there the LORD scattered them over the face of the whole earth* (Gen. 11:8–9).

The most well-known version of the diaspora story is, of course, that found in Genesis 11, the Tower of Babel. The basic plot tells us that mankind decided to "make a name" for itself by building a city "and a tower whose top is in the heavens."[1] God, seeing that the people's arrogant efforts were aided by their communication with each other, confused their language and "scattered them abroad from there over the face of all the earth."[2] Most people view this well-known myth as an attempt to explain the variance in languages around the world, making it a type of nature myth. A *lesser*-known part of the account, however, is found in the preceding chapter of Genesis, often called the "Table of Nations." In chapter 10, the descendants of Noah are listed, in some cases to the sixth generation after Noah. Many of these descendants can be identified with ancient nations. For example, Mizraim, Cush, and Canaan[3] can be identified with the regions of Egypt, Ethiopia, and Palestine, respectively.

What this implies is that as the descendants of Noah dispersed, many of them founded cities and kingdoms that ultimately bore the names of their founders. So Mizraim, Noah's grandson through Ham, founded a kingdom that became *known* as Mizraim — the Hebrew name for modern-day Egypt. Cush, in turn, founded a kingdom known as Cush — the ancient name for modern-day Ethiopia. And, of course, the "land of Canaan" is modern-day Palestine/Israel. Some even identify Meshech, grandson of Noah through his son Japheth, with the ancient name for Moscow (though this is still a widely debated point). In essence, what we find in this "Table of Nations" is that many of Noah's descendants are linked to specific countries and people groups.[4]

This is a perfectly reasonable idea. Even today in America, many of our historical sites bear the names of famous and well-known people of that time: *James*town, *William*sburg, *Penn*sylvania, and so forth.

While this does not *prove* the Genesis version, it certainly indicates that, if the Table of Nations is even *somewhat* accurate, *some form* of dispersion occurred. If we add to this dispersion the "confusion of languages," it is easy to imagine how the development of separate cultures around the world unfolded. We are told later that this division of languages — and henceforth cultures — happened during the time of

Peleg, Noah's great-great-great-grandson through his son Shem.[5]

The diaspora myth is often considered an attempt to explain the origins of other languages, but, in truth, it goes beyond that. While it does explain the origin of foreign languages, it also serves to narrate the history of a group of people after a catastrophic flood. It acknowledges that, after the cultures developed different languages, they began to scatter and divide, with like languages grouping together. Naturally, as these groups began to divide, newer dialects emerged, which soon became newer languages, driving further wedges between people groups. As more and more languages formed, more and more people began to segregate, forming more and more cultures. It is sort of a "linguistic natural selection," or a "birds of a feather flock together" mentality, which, I strongly believe, transforms it from a *nature* myth into an *event* myth. *This* is the basis for the telephone mythology theory. Why? In such a diaspora, we would expect *similar* stories to develop *different* details, because *one* central culture would fragment into *many* different cultures. However, this theory only works if the diaspora myth has credibility.

Does the mere *existence* of "The Great Dispersion Myth" in Genesis lend itself credibility? For some, that is enough. For others, however, they need something more substantial. To me, the myth only has credibility if it can *support itself* by showing evidence of having spread throughout various cultures. If a myth about the dispersion has, in effect, *dispersed* to other cultures, then it becomes a supportable theory. Now the question becomes: *does* it appear in other cultures? Fortunately, it does.

In Burma, for example, the Gherko Karens tell of a story in which the people decided to build a pagoda that would reach to heaven. Their god, in his wrath, came down, confused their language, and scattered the people about the earth.[6] In the

Congo, they balanced on poles, and in Mexico, they built a tower out of clay. Each of these versions tells of a god who becomes angry at their endeavors and scatters them abroad. In India, a Hindu legend tells of a group of demons that attempted to build an altar that would reach the sky, but whose completion was thwarted by Indra, the sky-god.[7]

And the parallels do not stop with just these aforementioned cultures. Indeed, the story is almost as universal as the story of the Deluge. In some cases, however, a particular culture contains only one element of the story. It may, for example, tell only of the construction of the tower, while leaving out the confusion of languages. For example, the Ba-Luyi, an African tribe in the Upper Zambesi region, tells of a great tower made of "masts" that, because of its instability, falls down and kills all who are involved in the project. The purpose for the tower is to reach the sun-god Nyambe,[8] though it is not Nyambe who punishes them. The destruction of their tower arises, instead, from the natural consequences of their actions. In a remarkably similar story from the Congo, it is said that the Wangongo wanted to see what the moon was, and so fastened one pole to another, until everyone in the village was climbing the poles. With that much weight, it is said that the tower suddenly collapsed and "since that time no one has tried to find out what the moon is."[9] These versions all have the thwarting of a construction project, but they lack the "confusion of tongues" element.

On the other hand, many cultures have the story of the confusion of tongues and the dispersion of people, but leave out the construction of a tower. The Greeks, for example, used to tell that the god Hermes separated mankind into different nations and introduced different types of speech. The action does not appear to be wrathful punishment, but merely a sort of divine practical joke. In Assam, the Kachcha Nagas told of a story in which a band of warriors, attacking a python, suddenly found themselves to be speaking different languages. "The men of the same speech," it says, "now drew apart from the rest and formed a separate band."[10]

If the myth is to have credibility, how do we account for so much variance? We account for it by applying telephone mythology. *If* a central culture experienced such a life-altering event as this diaspora, then we would expect the story to be passed down from generation to generation. It's what people do. It's why Independence Day is celebrated every July fourth in America, and Passover is still celebrated by the Jewish people today. In addition, as each culture separated from the others and began to develop its own set of beliefs and values, then we would expect the stories to change. Just like the telephone game, certain details get lost or added during the transmission. We see it today in the so-called urban legends. Though the stories are usually similar, some of the details change depending on where in the country you are. "Ghost lights," one of the more popular legends, is an excellent example of this.

The basic phenomenon is always the same: a bright ball of light inexplicably travels, usually at high speeds, down an open road or an abandoned railroad track. The phenomenon itself is incredibly well documented from all over the United States. Several counties in North Carolina experience them, as do many towns in the Midwest and western United States. In Richmond, Virginia, there is a location that often has these "ghost lights." The origin of the lights is officially attributed to either swamp gas or a form of lightning known as ball lightning, but that fact does not stop the numerous other "explanations" that have arisen. In some localities, the lights are said to be the spirits of departed souls. In other localities, they are said to be ghost trains. In still others, they are said to be the lanterns of dead railway men who wander the tracks, looking for something (a lost soul mate, their missing *heads*,[11] *etc.*). The numerous versions don't take away from the fact that the lights *do* exist

— again, they are too well documented — the explanations simply change to suit the location and storytellers. For ghost lights near old abandoned tracks, a railroad explanation is devised; scientists hold to swamp gas/lightning explanations; Civil War hospitals are evoked in the South. *The details change with the culture.*

This is all well and good, you may be asking, but why should we believe it? Isn't the conventional interpretation — that the stories are simply *fictional* tales — good enough? Why must we assume that the events depicted actually happened?

We would easily dismiss the stories as purely fictional if it were not for their *universality*. Yes, I would expect cultures to invent a myth explaining the existence of other cultures around them. That is logical. What is not logical is that almost every culture in the world would invent a *similar*, if not virtually *identical* myth, explaining the existence of other cultures. Because this story exists almost *everywhere*, what seems more probable is that the event *really happened*.

If, therefore, we take the stories of a diaspora as fact — not necessarily choosing one particular version over another, but simply acknowledging the spread of cultures after a deluge — then the various versions of the Flood (and a lot of other mythology, as well) begin to seem a little more reasonable. In fact, as we look at the various versions and begin to compare them to each other using telephone mythology, we begin to see that, not only does an actual global Deluge seem *possible,* it seems to be, at least from a literary standpoint, quite *probable.* In addition, to claim that the three versions were *carried* to their respective regions lends an amount of credibility to the story as a whole, because the story's *very claims are supported by its retelling*.

If the diaspora occurred, then the scattered people would have the same history. If they carried that history with them, they would retell the stories of their past. As the stories move further and further from the original source — in terms of both distance and time — we would expect the stories to change. However, because each version has its roots in the actual event, we would also look for a common core in the stories. This is precisely what we find in the diaspora myths. It's also what we find in the Deluge myths.

So now we look at the versions of the Flood themselves. Over the course of the next few chapters, we will examine several characteristics of the stories. First, we will look at the heroes. That is, we will examine the characteristics of the main character in each version. Then we will look at the rest of the passengers, as well as the cargo. We will look, as well, at the final resting place of the vessel and, lastly, the use of animals in the different versions of the myth. All of these common threads contain details that often seem quite at odds with each other, and have presented a problem for people trying to reconcile the various versions of the Deluge. Telephone mythology, however, helps us immensely in this endeavor.

We will be exploring this idea of telephone mythology by consulting several Deluge myths. Primarily, we will be looking at the *Mahābhārata*, the Kariña story of the Flood, and the Genesis account.[12] We will be considering, as well, Babylonian, Australian, and East Asian literature. Before we begin, however, I want to look briefly at the origins of our three primary sources. The differences in their styles are as vast as the differences between the cultures that produced them. This is what makes them so fascinating. It is also, perhaps, what enables their similarities to stand out so vividly.

Endnotes
1. Genesis 11:4; NKJV.
2. Genesis 11:8; NKJV.
3. Genesis 10:6.

4. In an interesting twist, Nimrod, great-grandson of Noah, built a city known as "Erech." The Gilgamesh Epic informs us that Gilgamesh was the "King of Erech."
5. Genesis 10:25.
6. Theodore Gaster, *Myth, Legend, and Custom in the Old Testament* (New York: Harper and Row Publishers, 1969), p. 135–136.
7. Ibid., p. 132–134.
8. Ibid., p. 132.
9. Ibid., p. 132–133.
10. C.A. Soppitt, *A Short Account of the Kachcha Nâga (Empêo) Tribe in the North Cachar Hills* (Schillong: The Assam Secretariat Press, 1885), p. 15.
11. Some versions actually tell that the lights are souls who, while alive, lost their heads in a terrible accident.
12. The three primary sources, in their totality, can be found in appendix A. The secondary sources can be found in appendix B.

Chapter 4

THE SOURCES

In days long-past, the sky-god, Kaputano,
came down to the kingdom of the Kariña.
— The Flood According to the Kariña

Part of the appeal of the Flood account is its widespread popularity among ancient cultures. It is found on every continent (with the exception of Antarctica, of course), in many different countries, and across a variety of people groups. These reasons alone are why I chose this particular myth. However, its prevalence did not mean my task was particularly easy. Because there are innumerable sources from which I could have drawn, selecting only three primary sources was far from simple. After much reading and studying, however, I finally settled on the Kariña, Jewish, and Hindu versions.

Geographically speaking, the three primary sources stand in stark contrast to each other. The Hindu myth — written in Sanskrit — was well-known throughout much of southeastern Asia. The Jewish myth — written in Hebrew and later translated into Greek — became widespread throughout much of the Middle East, spreading with its people through Egypt and Babylonia. The Kariña myth — told in an obscure Cariban dialect — was only popular with one particular tribe of Native South Americans who still live today in eastern Venezuela. Because the sources are so varied, the ideological frameworks in which we find each of these myths are vastly different, as well. We'll take a look at the cultural origins of each of these versions. In addition, I will give my reasons for selecting each legend as a primary source.

The Mahābhārata

The *Mahābhārata* is one of two great Sanskrit poems, an epic on par with the *Iliad* and the *Odyssey* of Greek mythology. It is one of the many sources from which Hindus draw an understanding of both their religion and their history. The poem itself deals primarily with a land dispute. Woven into the main story, however, are thousands of side stories and myths that teach a good deal of the history and belief of the ancient Aryan people.

The Aryans are referred to in several of the ancient Hindu works, most notably in a work known as the *Rig Veda*. The word *Arya*, means "noble" or "cultured" in Sanskrit. In the early 19th century, it became the long-standing assumption that the Aryans were European invaders that conquered the more primitive Dravidian people living in India at the time. However, the idea formed less from any evidence than from simple, unadulterated racism. The Europeans who conquered India in the late 18th and early 19th centuries simply assumed that such an intelligent and "noble" race *must* have come from

Europe, and could not have been indigenous to Asia. This idea of a vastly superior race of Europeans known as "Aryans" was the basis for Hitler's blond-haired, blue-eyed "Aryan race" that he was attempting to create during the Third Reich.

Now, as more and more — and older — references to the Aryans have cropped up in the past few decades, historians have been forced to abandon this idea of a superior invading race slaughtering inferior natives. It is currently believed, therefore, that the word simply references the earliest sages of India, known as the "Nobles" by later people. This is not unheard of. Even in America, we tend to refer to the "Founding Fathers" when we speak of the great minds that drafted the Constitution of the nation. In any event, within the *Mahābhārata* lay several stories that reveal the history and belief of that ancient culture.

The name of the book itself comes from two words, *mahā*, meaning "great" or "large," and *bhārata*, meaning "[battle of] the Bhāratas." The Bhāratas were a tribe in India that had eventually split into two clans: the Kurus and the Pāṇdus. At some point in time, the two clans began warring over a parcel of land that had belonged to their ancestors. By the time of the poem, the battle is over, the Kurus have been annihilated, and the Pāṇdus alone survive. The *Mahābhārata* is the story of the initial dispute, and the years leading up to the great battle.

The part of the story in which we are interested, "The Fish Story of Manu," is found in book III, chapter 185. It is told to the traveling Pāṇdus as they wander about the land, exiled, in the years before the battle. The story is related to the other Pāṇdus by Mārkaṇdeya, a member of their company.

In the original Sanskrit, the poem makes up roughly seven volumes. In English, that length nearly triples to 19 volumes.[1] The work is sprawling. It varies in vocabulary, grammar, style, and meter. It has been called a "literary monstrosity,"[2] and is an intellectual thicket of history and philosophy. Because of its sheer size and scope, we can hardly help but wonder how such an immense work came into being.

The origin of the *Mahābhārata* has been a point of debate for the last 200 years, when the work was first translated into English. The Sanskrit grammarian Pāṇini offered an etymological description of the title sometime around 400 B.C. Most Sanskrit literature references the work and even quotes it, indicating just how influential the epic poem has been. There is, however, one exception to the rule: the Vedic literature.

The *Vedas* are a collection of religious hymns composed over a large period of time (the *Rig Veda*, mentioned above, is one of these). No one is precisely sure when they were begun, but we do know that they were finally completed sometime between 1800 B.C. and 1400 B.C. Because of their religious nature, they should surely have been influenced by the *Mahābhārata*. However, they are not. In fact, they do not reference the poem at all, leading most people to believe that the *Mahābhārata* was not in existence at that point. This is a reasonable idea. Because the work is referenced by 400 B.C., though not referenced in 1400 B.C., we can safely assume it was written sometime within that window. Any actual *date* given within that window is, at this point, merely conjecture.

Who wrote the *Mahābhārata*? Tradition claims that one man, a sage named Vyāsa, composed the epic poem single-handedly. However, outside of this basic tradition, there is no way to confirm the "historicity" of this "mythological figure."[3] In other words, history cannot, so far, even confirm the *existence* of Vyāsa, let alone that he composed one of Hinduism's greatest works. If we add to it the sheer size and scope of the epic poem, we find it even more difficult to believe that one man composed the *Mahābhārata*. It seems far more likely that the work was composed over several centuries, based on oral tradition and previously existing documents. Interestingly, the name "Vyāsa" actually *means* "arranger" and "distributor," and so may not even be intended to refer to an actual *author* but is merely used as an indication that the poem was compiled (or "arranged") from many sources. However, dismissing the idea of a single author outright *is* rather unfair. Besides, regardless of how it came about, the *Mahābhārata* is an impressive work.

This version of the Flood has been translated by the author. I selected the Sanskrit version for two reasons. First, I wanted a version that I could, personally, translate. From a purely linguistic standpoint, I wanted to see with my own eyes that at least *one* version did claim the Flood to be global. Many arguments *against* the Deluge follow the lines that we are misinterpreting the literature, and I wanted to lay *that* argument to rest in my own mind. Secondly, I selected this version because it is *not* well-known in this country. Few people in America are even familiar with Sanskrit literature at all, let alone a Sanskrit myth buried within a much larger work, as is the case with the Fish Story and the *Mahābhārata*. Since I am a firm believer in learning to understand other cultures — even if we, ultimately, disagree with these other cultures — introducing a little-known piece of literature just seems like the right thing to do.

The Torah: Genesis

The Jewish Bible was written over a thousand-year span, from around 1400 B.C. to 400 B.C. In scope, it deals with the personal relationship of God with His people, the Hebrews (or Israelites). This basic theology is in sharp contrast with the polytheistic view of the *Mahābhārata*. In the Hindu literature, the many gods only become involved in human affairs when it is of greatest profit to them, whereas the Hebrew God shows a continued and vested interest in the well-being of the people of earth. The general theme of the Jewish Bible is, more or less, as follows:

1. God creates people.

2. People rebel against God.

3. God punishes those people.

4. God promises to provide a way out of that punishment (both now and in the afterlife) by sending a chosen being, a person known in Hebrew as *Messiah*, to rescue the people of earth from the punishment of their sins.

The Bible is known to have numerous authors, and because some of the books do not have a clear authorship, finding a precise number of contributors has been a difficult task over the years. Tradition says that the first five books (Genesis, Exodus, Leviticus, Numbers, and Deuteronomy) were written by Moses around 1400 B.C., during the 40-year span in the desert immediately following the Exodus from Egypt. The Books of Moses — as they are often called — make up the portion of the Jewish Bible known as the *Torah*, or "The Law." It is generally believed that Moses penned the books based solely on existing oral traditions; however, many argue that Moses merely compiled already existing manuscripts when he wrote the Book of Genesis. Over the years, some have even gone so far as to suggest that, by the time of the Exodus, Genesis was, more or less, already complete, and Moses merely "polished" the manuscript. It should be noted that though none of these scenarios can be either confirmed or disputed, the New Testament always refers to Moses as the writer (John 5:46; 2 Cor. 3:15).

The Book of Genesis deals with *origins*. It begins with the origin of mankind through his creation by the supreme God. From there, it tells of the origin of suffering and selfishness, and the corruption of humanity that ensues. It tells of other origins, such as language, music, and metallurgy. Eventually — some would say ultimately — it tells of the origin of the Hebrews and the nation that would become Israel.

The point of interest for us, the Flood of Noah, is found in chapters 6–9 of Genesis, the first book of the *Torah*. At this point, it is said that man has been on the earth for some 1,700 years, and his sin is so great that "every plan devised by his mind was nothing but evil all the time." Because of this consistent evil, God decides to destroy the earth, saving, of course, Noah, his three sons, and all four of the men's wives.

This version is taken from the *Tanakh*, the rabbinical version of the Torah translated by the Jewish Publication Society. I selected the story of Noah because it is the version with which most people are familiar, but it is also the most misunderstood version. For example, most people do not realize that the boat in this version is larger than 500 railway stock cars combined.[4] Many also forget that, in some cases, Noah was asked to bring, not 2 of each animal, but *14*.[5] Most of us probably remember that Noah brought the animals on "two by two." However, what many of us who grew up with the story have forgotten is that several of those animals came on "two by two, by two, by two, by two, by. . . ." All of this is to say, in short, that despite its familiarity, most people do not know the details of the Hebrew version. I wanted to provide a study of it in order to clear up many of the misconceptions regarding it.

The Kariña Peoples

The Kariña people, also known as the Carib Indians, were indigenous to eastern Venezuela and were among the first people the Spanish settlers met upon arriving on the South American continent. At that time, they were fisherman, farmers, and sailors . . . but they were also warriors. They were fierce fighters, often eating their prisoners, and succeeded in all but wiping out the Arawaks, a neighboring tribe. In fact, it's believed that the term "cannibal" originated out of a corruption of their name.

According to their own traditions, the Kariña were created from the bones of an enormous snake (or in some versions, a dragon). Historically and anthropologically, it is believed that the Kariña moved southward from the northern coast of South America, passing through the region of the Lesser Antilles. Eventually they settled in the valley between the Orinoco River and the eastern shore of Venezuela.

The Kariña believe in four distinct deities. The first, Ioroska, is the god of earth. He rules over ignorance, darkness, and death. It is Ioroska who, at the request of the village shamans, cures illnesses. Akodumo, the water-god, rules with his serpent spirits and controls all aquatic life. Akodumo is the Kariña version of Neptune.

The Kariña believe that the mountains are the connection between earth and heaven, and it is the mountain-god, Mawari, who rules over this axis with his vulture spirits. The last — and supreme — god is Kaputano, the sky god. After ascending to the sky, Kaputano took the form of Orion, where he now reigns as the highest-ranking omnipotent being. In their version of the Flood, it is Kaputano who warns the Kariña about the coming Deluge.

By the time of the Spanish settlement, the story of the Flood was already an established myth for them, and was first recorded in Fray Cesáreo de Armellada's work, *Indigenous Venezuelan Literatures*.[6] As with most of their stories, the legend was told in a strictly oral fashion, and was merely one of numerous other stories told around campfires at night. Today, the Kariña, who number around 11,000 people, still hold many of their ancient beliefs, including the story of the Flood.

The Kariña version is based on the book *The Great Canoe*, by Maria Elena Maggi. I have taken a few liberties in retelling it, but the core of the story, and certainly most of the details, remain the same. Maggi's version, published by Douglas & McIntyre, can be found in most bookstores. This particular version of the myth appealed to me because it is so far removed, geographically, from the other two versions, and I felt it would be interesting to look at a version of the story that would be clearly uninfluenced by other similar tales. And, as I mentioned before, it's always a good idea to introduce ourselves to a culture with which we may not be familiar. If any culture fits that bill in North America, it's the Kariña culture.

At this point, it is suggested that you turn to appendix A. There you will find the full versions of all three primary sources. Read them, get a minimal working knowledge of their details, and *then* continue on. You may wish to read the different versions in appendix B, as well, though we will tend to cover the necessary information as needed. You may or may not also wish to flip back and forth between the text and the stories as you continue on in the book; that is entirely up to you. However, I *strongly* recommend being at least somewhat familiar with the three primary versions before going any further.

Endnotes
1. B.A. Van Nooten, *The Mahābhārata* (New York: Twayne Publishers, Inc, 1971), p. 135–136.
2. Thus Maurice Winternitz, *History of Indian Literature* (Calcutta: University of Calcutta, 1963), p. 286.
3. Van Nooten, *The Mahābhārata* p. 43.
4. See chapter 11.
5. Genesis 7:2.
6. Maria Elena Maggi, *The Great Canoe: A Kariña Legend* (Toronto: Douglas and McIntyre, 1998), p. 33.

Chapter 5

THE FLOOD: TRAITS OF THE HERO

Exceeding the brilliance of his own father and grandfather with vigor, splendor, fortune, and, above all, piety, Manu the king, standing in the garden of penance on one foot with his extensive arms raised, performed completely and passionately the greatest of all pious rituals, the tapas. So with his head hung down and his eyes unblinking, he performed this frightful penance for a thousand years, bearing wet clothes and matted hair.
— *Mahābhārata*, book III, chapter 185, verses 3–6

The heroes in these stories all embody a rather intriguing mixture of human fallibility and divine perfection. We do not see the main characters revered as gods at any point in the stories. At the same time, we *do* see them presented with a "better-than-the-average-human" air. So which is it? Was the historical hero of the Flood a human or a demigod? Let's explore those questions in this chapter.

Genesis

Genesis dwells on the character of Noah for only a short while. In most translations, Noah is described in under 15 words. However, despite its brevity, the description is quite profound: "Noah was a righteous man; he was blameless in his age; Noah walked with God."

Righteous . . . blameless. . . . These are Hebrew terms that mean "holy," or "perfect."

Picturing a model of perfection is quite difficult, as we have no real frame of reference. After all, we certainly do not see perfect people walking around today! Indeed, the Jewish — and Christian — Bible indicates that there is no such thing as a blameless person.[1] The *Torah*'s consistent theme, in fact, is that God alone is righteous. As if to emphasize this point, even in the Genesis version we later see Noah drunk and naked in his tent sometime after the Flood.[2] This is hardly "righteous" or "blameless" behavior. Since God is omniscient, would He not have known of Noah's indiscretion when He called Noah "blameless"? Could He, then, truly consider Noah blameless? If Noah wanders from righteousness — another word for *blamelessness* — then he cannot rightfully be *called* "blameless."

Matthew Henry, noted biblical scholar and author of *Matthew Henry's Commentary on the Whole Bible*, writes that the patriarchs, despite being revered, *did* sin (quite often, in fact). He suggests that the author of Genesis left the incident there in order to show Noah's righteousness comes from his heart, instead of his actions. To put it a different way, it is Noah's intent that earns him the description: "Noah walked with God."

King David is often regarded as a "man after God's own heart,"[3] despite being an adulterer, a murderer, and a lousy father. Why? In his heart he pursued righteousness. His son, Solomon, actually describes his father as being "righteous *at heart*."[4] Noah appears to fit into this same category. Although Noah physically falls from the perfect image of "righteousness," God still considers him righteous enough to survive the Flood.

The Mahābhārata

Half a world away in India, the story of Manu resonates with this idea of being blameless in intent, if not always in action. In the beginning of the Sanskrit story, we find Manu possessing the Hindu version of righteousness. He is full of "vigor, splendor, fortune, and, above all, piety." Unlike the story of Noah, however, the story of Manu *demonstrates* these qualities for us. We are told in the text that Manu performs the *tapas* for an extremely *long* period of time: a thousand years.

Tapas is translated, literally, as "fire." However, it actually has two meanings in Hinduism (neither of which refers to the Mediterranean appetizer platters found in trendy restaurants). First, it is the "creative energy" of the body — essential body heat, metabolism, and so forth. Secondly, *tapas* is a term that refers to the performance of meditation and severe austerities. Through this performance of *tapas*, one can learn to control the creative energy of *tapas*, using it for power and for connecting to the "divine intelligence that orchestrates the universe."[5] It has, in effect, then, a double meaning. By performing the *act of tapas*, one can control the *tapas force* within oneself.

An example of this is found in the *Atharva Veda*. In this V*eda*, we read *yad agne tapasā tapa upatapyāmahe tapa*: the fire-god Agni *creates* tapas *by means of* tapas.[6] In other words,

Agni creates the *energy form* of *tapas* by means of the *tapas process*. In both cases, *tapas* is used to gain and control power. It is, simply, a power within itself, but it can also be used and harnessed to *create* more power. It reminds me of the law of conservation of energy, which states that energy cannot create itself, but must come from an *external* energy source. *Tapas*, as a power, is created by *tapas*, the act, which then enables the yogi to harness more of the *tapas* power to further continue performing the act of *tapas*.

The *tapas* ritual has long been considered a measure of sincerity, holiness, and spiritual power. The Hindu guru Shiva Bala Yogi is rumored to have performed *tapas* for 12 years, attaining the ability to move objects with his mind, project his spirit elsewhere, and to surround himself with a constant humming sound, identified as the *aum* of Hindu meditation.[7] We may or may not believe that to be true, and whether it is true or not is beside the point. The *point* is that we are told in the *Mahābhārata* that it is through a similar form of rigorous *tapas* refinement that Manu earns the right to survive the Flood.

We do not see Manu's fallibility until the end of the tale (just as in the story of Noah), when he becomes "bewildered" during the process of re-creating the world. In the Hindu ideology, to become "bewildered" is to lose one's way in the cosmic path of one's calling; it is a sign that one is weighed down by the fetters and chains of the self. You see, to the Hindu mind, humans are born divine. It is only after becoming attached to the things of this world that we lose our divinity — our connection to the god Brahma. The practice of *tapas*, to the Hindus, is one of the pathways back to this lost divinity — one of the *yogas*. It is what allows Manu to begin the selfless and holy act of recreating life. Thus, where giving and creating life is a self*less* act, to allow oneself to be interrupted is a self*ish* act, as it prevents a good deed by allowing the mind to become distracted. Manu, in other words, enters a brief period of mental darkness that breaks his selfless act, disconnecting him from the righteousness he had "attained." This is the Hindu version of lying drunk and naked in a tent (though I am not all that certain Noah's behavior would be condoned in Hinduism, either).

Flaws: Added Realism?

Why are these particular flaws pointed out in the text? If we are to believe the idea that these people survive this hardship because of their holiness, then why bother presenting flaws in the hero at all? Why not cast aside the imperfections and fully exalt the heroes of these myths, particularly if we're to *view* them as exalted heroes? Many mythologists argue that these details are often added as an afterthought, in order to make the stories believable to a gullible audience. While this is, indeed, *possible*, it is certainly not *probable*.

Other divine heroes exist in comparable mythology. The Jews who wrote the New Testament, for example, center the focus of their writings on the divinely perfect Savior found in the person of Christ — using that perfection as testimony to back up their claims that He is Messiah. The ancient Greeks consistently created human characters that were also, at least in part, of divine blood (e.g., Hercules and Phaëthon). In Sanskrit mythology, Krishna is said to be, not the first, but the *ninth* human incarnation — the *avatara* — of the god Vishnu. In essence, enough divine humans exist in mythology that there is no need to claim that character flaws make a fictional protagonist more believable, because there are enough protagonists *without* character flaws. Taking an Eastern approach, in fact, we see the idea of divinity in humans to be far more prevalent and commonplace than in a Western, Judaic view. In Western literature, most people are simply people, with the rare few that appear to supersede mere humanity. In the Eastern literature, it is the opposite; divine humans are almost the norm. So we must ask ourselves again: why bother with this humanity if the storytellers are knowingly composing fictional accounts? Why not claim the characters are gods and be done with it, as this is what so often happens anyway? Why stress their *flaws* if we are to believe that they are more *righteous* than we are?

What seems most likely is that the stories actually refer to a *real* human, someone who is virtuous — at least in intent — but still human. In both the Sanskrit and Hebrew versions, this fallible humanity is overlooked because of the *relationship* that each hero has with his Creator. Despite his falling away from divinity — remember, in Hinduism, humans are born divine but only lose that divinity after they become distracted by the things of this world — Manu maintains the *tapas* he needs to re-create the world. Despite his eventual drunken exhibitionism, Noah is still considered "blameless."

In the vein of Moses (a murderer),[8] and Arjuna (a deserter),[9] the heroes of the Flood have managed, despite their shortcomings, to earn the care and respect of their God. In the Hebrew text, Noah survives because of his *relationship* with God. In the Sanskrit text, Manu earns survival first through *piety*, then through his *relationship* with Brahma. In the Kariña legend, it is because of *fear* and *trust* that the people survive. The Montagnais literature recalls an angry god who commands an *obedient* man to build a vessel. For the Hareskin Indians, *wisdom* is the attribute that allows the hero to survive the Deluge. In each of these versions, the virtuous are saved from a terrible judgment, and the obedient, the pious, and the God-fearing people outlive corrupt humanity.

Walking with God. Piety. Fear. Trust. Obedience. Wisdom. What should spring immediately to mind is that all of these traits are interrelated. A man who is blameless and walking with God would, by necessity, respect and honor the Creator with whom he walked. With that respect, we would expect to find an attitude of obedience, as well as a desire to please through "moral" behavior. These different traits may not be describing different people at all. Rather, they may very well be describing the *same* person. In that case, you may ask, if each story refers to the same person, why are *different* aspects chosen to describe him? Why is one "pious" and another "obedient"? Why are they not all described as obedient, pious, blameless people? Manu performs the *tapas*, while Noah is simply called "blameless." The Kariña are not described at all, but simply do as they are told, indicating that their virtue lies in their *obedience*. If the heroes all refer to the same person, then *why do the descriptions differ?*

The breakdown occurs as the story begins to spread throughout the re-developing cultures of the diaspora. Each culture develops its own idea of what is necessary for salvation in the story. For the Hebrews, a personal relationship with the Creator is of the utmost importance. For the Hindus, a clear mind formed by continual ascetic practices is of the utmost importance. Some cultures teach *unquestioning* devotion, and for others, fear brings pleasure to their god. As such, the developing cultures are going to select, in their re-telling of the event, the *characteristics that most fit within their ideological framework*. Yet while the traits are all different, they are still *interrelated*.

To condense and simplify this, we can make the following summary: the man who worships his Creator to the fullest intent possible would contain all of these elements that we find broken down in the various stories. Running these traits backward through the diaspora, we can easily surmise that one man served as the inspiration for the various heroes in the re-told stories.

Thus we see the first example of telephone mythology put into practice with our heroes. Each of these characters — Noah, Manu, and the unnamed Kariña people — possesses the characteristics relevant to their respective cultures. Likewise, these characteristics — piety, a desire to follow God, and obedience — may, in fact, all stem from one historical figure.

Now we will take a look at the other characters on board the ship. In most of the versions, one family — sometimes several families — boards the vessel with the hero, helping him to load and manage the cargo. Are there similarities between the crew in these versions? Are there differences? More importantly, can we *explain* those differences with telephone mythology?

Endnotes
1. Psalm 14:1–3, Romans 3:10.
2. Genesis 11:21.
3. 1 Samuel 13:14; Acts 13:22.
4. Cf. 1 Kings 3:6, emphasis added.
5. Deepak Chopra, *The Seven Spiritual Laws of Yoga* (Hoboken, NJ: John Wiley & Sons, Inc.), p. ix.
6. Walter O. Kaebler, *Tapa Mārga: Asceticism and Initiation in Vedic India* (New York: State University of New York Press, 1989), p. 2.
7. "Shiva Bala Yogi: Journal 7 — Tapas." www.shiva.org/jo7tapas.htm. ShriShivabalayogi Maharaj International Trust, 2001.
8. Exodus 2:11–12.
9. Stephen Mitchell, trans. *Bhagavad Gita*, (New York: Harmony Books, 2000), p. 43.

Chapter 6

THE FLOOD: THE CREW

"There, with the seven Ṛsis, sit, Great Manu."
— *Mahābhārata* Book III, chapter 185, verse 30

The crew of the ship is perhaps the strongest link we can find among the three primary versions. The link is so strong that we hardly even need to apply telephone mythology to this portion of the story. In fact, were it not for the secondary versions, we would *not* need to apply telephone mythology at all. The details — specifically the number of the crew members — are so comparable that we can surmise that the stories *must* have the same origin. However, outside of these primary sources there *is* some variance, and what we find is that — even when the details differ greatly

— telephone mythology is still of some use. Telephone mythology is, in fact, an arguably *necessary* application when it
comes to studying the crew.

The Crew According to the Mahābhārata

In the Fish Myth of the *Mahābhārata*, Manu is instructed
to take seven very specific people on board. While in many
versions the hero boards with his friends and family, Manu
boards the vessel with seven relatively obscure people — the
seven Ṛsis.[1]

The Ṛsis stem from the early period of Hinduism known
as the *Vedic* period (it is believed that the Vedas were developing during this time, hence the name). In Hindu mythology,
the Ṛsis are the seven "enlightened beings" who have been
granted knowledge of the Universal Truth. The *Rig Veda* says
they are "versed in ritual and meter, in hymns and rules."[2] They
are considered wise, pious, and holy. Because of this, the Ṛsis,
throughout the literature, exercise a wide influence on other
people, and often appear in stories as some sort of "mystic
sages," usually as stock characters. In fact, you might say that
they are a form of *Deus Ex Machina*, showing up whenever a
"wise, just sage" is needed. In some of the legends, the Ṛsis
are more supernatural than natural. In other legends, they
are simply wise humans. The literature fails to explain how
they came to posses their enlightenment, only that they have
always had this ancient knowledge. This particular story, unfortunately, does not really help to illuminate any of the mys-
tery surrounding the Ṛsis. It does not even bother to explain
their purpose on board. However, in spite of all of the unan-
swered questions we may have in regards to the Ṛsis, we *do*
know that they are highly regarded as leaders.

Brahma instructs Manu to "sit . . . [in the vessel] with the
seven Ṛsis." It is not Manu's family or friends, but these seven
companions who accompany Manu during his voyage. What

is so important about these seven passengers? For the purposes of this book, our interest lies in the fact that Manu sets off with *seven* companions. Remember that number . . . it will show up later.

The Crew According to Genesis

In the case of the *Torah*, Noah's companions are almost, but not quite, as obscure. While the text does not tell us much in regard to their characters, they are at least *identified* for us: his wife, three sons — Shem, Ham, and Japheth — and his three daughters-in-law. Besides this identification, though, we know very little of these passengers. What we do know is mostly inferred: they were probably found equally as "favorable before God," because they, too, were spared from the Deluge.

The *Torah* tells us nothing whatsoever of the character of Noah's wife. In a similar vein, what we know of the sons comes only from the list of genealogy given in chapter 10 of Genesis.[3] The importance here, however, lies in their number: three men and four women. Noah's wife and his six children total seven persons on board with the hero. Could the seven crew members of Noah's Ark and the seven "enlightened ones" of Manu's ship represent the same people? Add in the heroes of both versions and the total crew of both vessels numbers eight . . . the only eight people in the world "holy" enough to escape the Flood. Is this a *probable* interpretation? Maybe. Is it a *possible* interpretation? Definitely.

The Crew According to the Kariña

The Kariña version of the Flood does not identify the travelers specifically, but only tells us that they are "four couples" who are afraid of the coming judgment. While I am certainly no mathematician, I can see that "four couples" is, of course, eight people. I can also tell that this matches the number of people in both the Sanskrit and Hebrew texts. While it is, of course, *possible* that three separately developing cultures can fabricate the exact same detail, is it likely? Is it likely that three distinctly different people groups develop a story — whether by invention or misunderstanding — and put the *exact same number of people on the vessel*? It seems to ask for a greater stretch of the imagination to believe *that* hypothesis than it does to believe in an actual Deluge.

What if, however, the crew members differ in number from each other? What does that mean for the story? Would we be forced to throw out the legend as nothing more than a fable? Are there even differences? For those of us who believe the Flood was a historical event, we must admit that it would be extremely convenient if every version of the Flood from around the world had eight people on board each vessel. Unfortunately, as it turns out, there is a wide range of passengers. Thankfully, however, telephone mythology may come to the rescue.

Other Versions

In Upper Burma, the Chingpaws tell that the survivors of the Flood are only two people, a brother and a sister. From this brother and sister spring all the races of mankind after the Flood. In New Guinea, it is also said that only two survive the Deluge, though these two are not brother and sister. The Greek version of Deucalion and Pyrrah also has the crew consisting of two people (though some versions of the Greek story place their unnumbered "children" on board, as well). In Brazil, however, it is *four* people who survive by building a canoe.[4]

So which is it? Does the crew consist of *two* people, *four* people, or *eight* people? Can we determine the correct number, or should we give up? Obviously, we can turn to telephone mythology to explain the *difference* between the numbers. As we have seen before, the stories would change as they were passed down from generation to generation. This much is understandable. But the question now becomes: why would *this particular detail* change? Why would the different versions not retain the same number of passengers? Can we use telephone mythology to explain the *origins* of the different numbers?

From a strictly logical sense, if we are to expect the world to be repopulated by a small group of people, then the largest group possible makes sense. On the other hand, logically, the smallest group of survivors makes little to no sense at all. So, were we to order the number of survivors from "most likely true" to "least likely true," it would look like this:

1. Eight survivors, being most likely
2. Four survivors, being possible, but unlikely
3. Two survivors, being not likely at all

We would not reasonably expect a repopulation of the earth from simply one couple (though many of the creation myths have only one couple populating the earth to begin with, but that is an entirely different study). Likewise, it calls for a stretch of the imagination to expect only two couples to repopulate the earth. Four couples, however, seems like a somewhat feasible number. If we were to pick one of the groups, the best choice would seem to be the largest group possible. Therefore, for the time being, let us fully acknowledge that four couples were on board the actual, historical vessel. While it should be obvious that telephone mythology can account for the *decrease in numbers*, it does leave us with at least one major question: why would a culture feel it *justifiable* to decrease the number of survivors, particularly when that decrease makes little sense?

I feel it likely that *aspects* of the story changed simultaneously. Perhaps — and this is merely a guess — the number of crew members *decreases* as the supernatural influence in the story *increases*. In other words, with the reduction in numbers, we find the divine re-creation aspect creeping up more and more often. In the Chingpaw version mentioned above, the brother and sister have a child together. The child is then torn to pieces by an evil elf-witch, and it is from the scattered blood droplets of the child that the "rest of mankind springs." In the Greek version, it is stones that turn to other men and women. In the first, the human race must spring *from* the surviving couple (albeit in a gruesome and horrifying way). In the second version, inanimate objects are given life *by* the surviving couple. So, you see, we find supernatural involvement in the repopulating aspect *increasing*. The first version requires something *natural* to occur before the *super*natural can occur. The second version skips straight to the "magic," so to speak.

This is all interesting, but it becomes more interesting, because the progression of supernatural re-creation does not just happen in the secondary sources; it happens in our primary sources, as well. In the Hebrew version, the post-diluvian life survives the Flood without any supernatural re-creation. In the Kariña myth, eight people (four couples) survive the Flood. Though we are not told whether or not Kaputano re-creates humans, he *does* re-create the natural world, a detail not appearing in the *Torah*. In the Hindu version, despite the fact that there are eight people on board, we are told that Manu re-creates *everything* . . . including people.

There is a progression here. We move from *no* supernatural re-creation, to *some* supernatural re-creation, to *more powerful* supernatural re-creation. I wonder if, at the same time, we also move to fewer survivors on the vessels. As the number of survivors in the telling decrease, the need for "magic" would increase. On the flip side, if the original, historical vessel had only two people on board, and the retellings increased that number, then we can plausibly expect the retellings to decrease the amount of "divine intervention."

This is not, admittedly, a rock-solid theory. In order for that to be the case, we would have to *prove* that the changes occur simultaneously; we would have to prove that the earliest versions of the Flood story told contained no divine recreation, that later versions all developed some form of divine re-creation, and that still later versions finally submitted the re-population of the earth *wholly* to divine recreation. Moreover, we would have to demonstrate a true progression from eight survivors to two survivors in these versions. Because of this, please understand that I am not attempting to tell you how the changes in the story *definitely* developed, but I am merely attempting to tell you how the changes in the story *possibly* developed. Further research on this particular topic may lend credibility to the theory. Until that time, please remember that it is *only a theory*, and further work can confirm or refute this.

Having looked at the crew, now let us turn to the cargo. In the Sanskrit version, Manu brings only seeds, whereas Noah and the Kariña bring both seeds and animals. Which version is correct? Were there animals, or were there *not* animals? This is an awfully large detail to omit (or add). At first glance, it seems almost irreconcilable, but is it really?

Endnotes
1. Pronounced: *rē'shēz*
2. *Rig Veda*, Book X, Hymn 6, verses 6-7
3. See chapter IV.
4. Theodore Gaster, *Myth, Legend, and Custom in the Old Testament* (New York: Harper & Row, 1969), p. 125.

Chapter 7

THE FLOOD: THE CARGO

> *When they were done, they went about gathering two of each animal to put on board. They also brought seeds from every plant on earth.*
> — The Flood according to the Kariña

For many, the varying details of the cargo in the different versions of the myth are difficult to reconcile. Indeed, the vast differences found among the versions are, perhaps, the greatest cause for skepticism. These differences, though, may only be surface-deep and not nearly as great as we first believe. Like the variance in the crew of the vessels, the variance in the cargo *may* be easily explained.

The Cargo According to the Mahābhārata

Manu is instructed to stock the vessel with a collection of all of the seeds from around the world. The seeds are strictly brought as food for both him and the Ṛsis, as Manu takes neither beast nor plant aboard. Why did Manu not bring anything else on board? As we discussed earlier, Manu's *tapas* is sufficient for the re-creation of both plant and wildlife; his piety acts as a supernatural agent of creation. This does two things: first, it minimizes the cargo needs of the ship. Second, it renders the seeds unnecessary for replanting, as Manu would — at least presumably — have re-created plant life as well. Thus it is a fairly safe assumption that Manu and his seven companions sustained themselves on only a diet of seeds during the years on the ship.

Could there have been another use for the seeds? Not that we can tell, unless some of the seeds were planted on board the ship, and the plants were also used for food. This actually seems quite possible; the idea of Manu and the Ṛsis spending several years on the ocean with nothing to eat but seeds sounds a bit on the bleak side. On the other hand, this was not a luxury cruise but a survival scenario, so planting may not have been an option. In either case, Manu and the Ṛsis stock the ship with only seeds, and nothing else.

The Cargo According to Genesis

Noah's cargo, on the other hand, fits with his character: although he is righteous at heart, he is not bestowed with any "divine" powers and abilities. Like his character flaw, this detail was not likely to have been added for any realism, as the Hebrew author could have easily portrayed God as working *through* Noah to re-create life. An example of that in other Hebrew scriptures would be Moses. Moses is portrayed in the Book of Exodus as turning a staff into a serpent and the Nile into blood, because God is working *through* him.

Samson destroys the Philistine temple because of physical strength bestowed upon him by *God's* presence. We do not see this with Noah. Rather, from a very practical standpoint, Noah has to do all the work himself without any special divine powers.

Noah is instructed to bring not just the animals but also "everything that is eaten" as food for himself, his family, and the animals. After the Flood, Noah and his family are told simply to come out of the ark with the animals and "be fruitful and increase in number upon it" (Gen. 8:17). In the Hebrew version, neither God nor Noah re-creates life. Therefore, any leftover seeds were more than likely planted in order to bring forth vegetation. As it turns out, however, replanting may not have actually been necessary.

The Hebrew word translated "flesh" in chapter 6, verse 13, is the word *beheme*, which refers only to nostril-breathing land vertebrates in general. The word *remes*, translated as "creeping things," refers most often to reptiles, and appears as well. This indicates two things. First, in the Genesis version, the only animals Noah brought aboard the vessel would have been nostril-breathing land vertebrates. Second, the only animals God said He would destroy completely would have been these nostril-breathing land vertebrates (see also 7:22). Therefore plants would not necessarily have been destroyed completely. In addition, as many have noted, the dove brought back an olive branch, indicating re-growth had already occurred. So it's easy to assume that the seeds were merely meant — as in the case with Manu — as food, and nothing more. Unlike Manu, though, Noah must bring along seeds for food *and* he must bring animals. Where Manu re-creates life, Noah must bring it on board with him. However, again, *both* men are instructed to carry seeds for food.

The Cargo According to the Kariña

In the Kariña myth, the survivors are told to stock the Great Canoe with two of every animal and "a seed from every kind of plant." These details recall — some would say *parallel* — the Jewish myth beautifully. The re-creation happens in this myth as well, calling to mind the Hindu version, but it is the god Kaputano who re-creates life, and not the survivors of the Flood. An interesting idea presented in the Kariña myth is the idea that Kaputano, the deity who sends the Flood, also helps to build the canoe *and* becomes part of the crew. This idea is reflected in the Hindu myth where Brahma physically steers and guides the ship through the "disordered earth" (some have suggested the Hebrew version implies this, as well, because the word "remembered" in Genesis 8 may mean, more literally, "to take care of"). In the Kariña myth, the seeds are not for replanting, nor are they used for re-creation. They are merely included as a food supply (again similar to both the Hebrew and Sanskrit versions).

This version does raise an interesting question: why did the Kariña need so much food? In the Hebrew myth, Noah is in the ark for 375 days, and in the *Mahābhārata*, Manu is on the ocean for several years. For these accounts, a large supply of food would be necessary for survival. In the Kariña account, however, the Flood lasts only a few days. If that were the case, why would such an abundant supply of food be necessary? The next section deals with that question.

Synthesis

In essence, we see three parallels in these stories. The first parallel we see is between the Sanskrit and Kariña texts, where the earth must be re-created after the Flood. In the Sanskrit text, it is mostly animal and plant life that must be re-created. In the Kariña myth, the animals survive, but Kaputano creates the rest of the world fresh and new —

mountains, marshes, trees, and so on. This re-creation is not in the Hebrew version, but its presence indicates either that the Hebrew version *lost* that particular detail, or the other versions *added* that detail later on. Either way, its inclusion in these two versions indicates more than coincidence.

Secondly, we see the inclusion of animals in the Hebrew and Kariña texts. What is interesting about this particular detail is that it is included in a version in which a god — Kaputano, in this case — *does* re-create the world. Because Kaputano re-creates the earth, it is relatively unnecessary, from an imaginative standpoint, to include animals on board. The detail in the Kariña account is unnecessary. If I were inventing a story in which a deity re-creates the earth, I would *not* include animals on board. Rather, I would simply have them re-created along with everything else. Does this imply that, perhaps, the original historical Flood *actually* had animals on board? It most certainly does, and we will see more of this later on.

Lastly, in all three versions the seeds are used merely for food. In *not one* of these three versions *are the seeds used for replanting*. Why not? If we were inventing a story that we were attempting to pass off as truth, would it not make sense to have the crew plant leftover seeds? That would only seem logical. However, if we are dealing with an actual event rather than a well-planned and thought-out story, then some of the details may not make sense. *Particularly if this story is being passed down and retold.* One of these details that we looked at earlier — the amount of seeds present in the Kariña version — deserves a little more of our focus. The question we raised earlier regarding it is still a valid question: why would they need so many seeds?

Frankly, they wouldn't. What seems most plausible is that this particular detail — the detail of carrying seeds on board — has survived the diaspora long after the particular telling of the myth no longer required it. Where many unimportant details are abandoned ("unimportant" from the perspective of the narrating culture), the existence of a seemingly inane detail suggests an actual purpose for its inclusion in the first place. Why would the Kariña include such a detail unless it had been passed down to them? Furthermore, why would it have been passed down to them unless, at some point, the story required its inclusion? Could this also explain the inclusion of animals in the Kariña text? Why are there animals on board if Kaputano re-creates the earth?

It reminds me of the story of the Christmas ham. The story goes something like this: a young newly married man and his bride were having their first Christmas dinner. The man watched as his wife dutifully cut the ends off the ham before placing it in the roasting pan. When questioned as to why she would do such a wasteful thing, the woman replied, "It's how my mom always cooked the ham." That night, when the girl's parents came to dinner, the young man asked his mother-in-law why she always cut the ends off the ham before placing it in the oven. His mother-in-law thought a moment and then replied, "It's what *my* mother always did."

A prosperous and exciting year passed, and the young couple was to have Christmas dinner at her parents' house. To the young man's delight — for the ham situation, as he called it, was troubling him still — the girl's grandmother was there. As should be expected, during the course of the evening as the family was enjoying the baked but end-less ham, the young man asked the elderly matron about the curious tradition. The old woman stared at him for a long time before finally replying, "Because my pan wasn't big enough for the whole thing."

Long after the details are unnecessary for that particular version, they still appear. This is telephone mythology at work. Details remain, though they no longer make sense, and other details are distorted because the original telling no longer fits the "newer" versions. Why, if Kaputano is going to re-create everything, do the people need to bring animals? Why, if they are only on the waters for a few days, do they need such an abundant supply of food? These details only make sense if they had been passed down from earlier — perhaps more accurate — versions. Though the pans are now large enough, the ends of the ham are still removed. Though the length of the voyage is much shorter, the food supply hasn't been reduced. Such is the case in many of these details.

The Hareskin tribe of North America tells of an old man who builds a raft and collects the drowning animals two by two as he floats past them. This idea of a post-diluvian rescue is also found thousands of miles away in Victoria, Australia, where the aborigines in the Lake Tyers region tell of a pelican that journeys about in a canoe, collecting the refugees. Why is this detail not found in every version? Because the changing cultures either required its presence, *or* required its absence; the detail was either added or taken away later on, and the newer versions passed on the newer details. Animals are kept on board, seeds (but not plants) are used for food, and animals are rescued after the Flood starts, rather than before. In short, the story changes to suit the tellers.

One of the final aspects of the story to which we will turn is the final resting place of the vessel. If there were a Flood vessel, where would we expect to find it? In the mountains? On the plains? Which plain? Which mountain? Has the vessel been found, or would locating it be virtually impossible? Many have suggested that, after several thousand years of weather and possible dismantling, nothing would be left. The next chapter looks at this difficult problem.

Chapter 8

THE FLOOD: THE RESTING PLACE OF THE VESSEL

The waters flooded the earth for a hundred and fifty days. But God remembered Noah and all the wild animals and the livestock that were with him in the ark, and he sent a wind over the earth, and the waters receded. Now the springs of the deep and the floodgates of the heavens had been closed, and the rain had stopped falling from the sky. The water receded steadily from the earth. At the end of the hundred and fifty days the water had gone down, and on the seventeenth day of the seventh month the ark came to rest on the mountains of Ararat. The waters continued to recede until the tenth month, and on the first day of the tenth month the tops of the mountains became visible (Gen. 7:24–8:5).

Mountains. There is something majestic about them; their very presence commands our attention. They inspire a combined emotion of fear and breathless awe. It's the beauty of a city skyline mixed with the grandeur of the ocean. Perhaps it is their height as they rise above the surrounding landscape that does it. Perhaps it is the fact that they are solid — that their foundations are so secure. Perhaps it is also why the mountains are almost universally known as the final resting place of the Flood vessel.

This is not to say, however, that locating the final resting place of the vessel, based solely on the literature, is an easy task. Each account gives a different name to the resting place, and many accounts do not even *name* the mountain. In a handful of the versions, the mountains do not even come into play. How, then, are we to determine which mountain is correct? Can we? Or should we believe, as some have suggested, that the mountains in the different versions are merely *symbols* of something else, inspired and selected purely because of their majesty?

Ararats of the World

"The mountains of Ararat . . ." (Gen. 8:4). Located in Turkey, the Ararat range has overlooked the lands of numerous societies and empires: Babylon, Greek traders, the Roman Empire, and, of course, the Jews, to name just a handful of the many peoples that have walked in the shadows of this mountain range. During the writing of the Hebrew text, Mesopotamia was a thriving civilization, Nineveh was the capital of the great Assyrian Empire, and Babylon was slowly climbing the imperial ladder.

For decades, enthusiasts have been searching the slopes of Mt. Ararat in Turkey — specifically the area around the Ahora Gorge, on the southeastern side of the mountain — for the vessel known as Noah's ark. These searches have been encouraged in part by a World War I pilot who claims to have seen a large boat-like structure on the side of the mountain. The pilot, Lieutenant Roskovitsky of the Russian Imperial Air Force, was on a mission to observe Turkish troop movement throughout the region in early 1916. He and his co-pilot noticed what appeared to be the hull of a ship sticking out from a glacial lake on the southeastern side of the mountain. The other part of the ship was buried under the water. Since Roskovitsky's now discredited report of the incident, numerous groups have trekked up the mountain over the years attempting to catch a glimpse of "Noah's ark." All that remains, however, are questionable accounts and grainy radar images.

Unfortunately, what makes these accounts so questionable is that, first and foremost, they contradict each other. In a few versions, the vessel is, more or less, intact, while in others it has been dismantled in places and the wood carted off. In some, the vessel is half-submerged in a glacial lake, while in others, it is protruding from the side of the mountain, half-buried in the snow that covers Mt. Ararat nine months out of the year. In Roskovitsky's account, the vessel is leaning on its side, while later accounts tell that the ark is standing straight up, allowing some of the explorers to walk along the top of it. Had this been the other way around, I might be a little less skeptical. In other words, had the earlier accounts told of the vessel standing up, and later on the vessel had "keeled over," I could believe it. I cannot, however, believe that the vessel would *fight gravity* and *right itself*.

Secondly, no one has been able to bring back clear photographs of the "ark." Many have tried, but cameras have either been lost, film stolen, or — more alarmingly — the photographer fell off the mountain and, perishing, took the only film with him. Even the photographs sent back to Tsar Nicholas II in early 1917 by a team of Russian engineers never made it to their final destination.[1] So we have basically two problems. First, the eyewitnesses cannot agree on what the object even *looks* like, or even how it is positioned on the mountain. Second, *no one* can provide proof of even *one* of the existing contradictory claims. Not *one clear photograph* has ever been produced, and the only images furnished are fuzzy radar images taken from 500 miles away. The images, at best, show a dark, box-like smudge on the side of the mountain, but it is impossible to tell if the smudge is man-made or merely a rock outcropping. There is, therefore, little evidence to suggest that the Flood vessel resides here. In fact, based *solely* on eyewitness accounts, I am inclined *not* to believe the vessel is on Mt. Ararat. I am not alone, for many have noted that Genesis reports that the ark came to rest on the "*mountains of Ararat*," not Mt. Ararat itself.

One last objection to the vessel residing on Mt. Ararat involves the volcanic and glacial activity on the mountain. Ararat is an active volcano. Though the last eruption was in 1840, the eruption and subsequent earthquakes were destructive enough to completely erase the village of Ahora and carve out the Ahora Gorge, *where the ark is supposedly located*. It calls for an extreme stretch of the imagination to expect the ark to survive some 3,000 years of weather, let alone the volcanic activity that affects the area.

In the Sanskrit version, we are told that Manu's boat landed on the peak of Mt. Naubandhanam. What we know about the resting place comes only from the text: it is called "the highest peak of the Himalayas." Today, the highest peak is known as Mt. Everest, in English, but has gone by the Hindi name of *Sagarmatha* for centuries. In fact, I have been unable to locate any existing record of the name *Naubandhanam* outside of the *Mahābhārata*. The *Atharva Veda*, written several centuries before the *Mahābhārata*, does refer to one of the summits in the Himalayas as *Navaprabhramsana*, which means "Gliding Down of the Ship."[2] However, this name, too, is not found outside of the literature. It seems that history, for now at least, has lost the location of Manu's mountain.

The Gilgamesh Epic, containing one of the other better-known versions of the Flood myth, was written around 600 B.C. and stored in the library at Nineveh. In the epic, the hero, Gilgamesh, speaks with the survivors of a deluge. The survivors tell him that the vessel has come to rest on the peak of Mt. Nişir. Nişir, like Naubandhanam of the Sanskrit version, has an obscure past.

Many claim that *Nişir* is simply the Babylonian name for Ararat, though this claim has little to no supporting evidence. Traditionally, Mt. Nişir is located in the modern-day Zagros Range of Iran. During the reign of the Assyrian King Ashurbanipal (883–859 B.C.), Mt. Nişir referred to a mountain now known as Mt. Cudi,[3] and some claim that it is on *this* mountain that the tomb of the Flood hero is said to be located.[4] However, the so-called Tomb of Noah does not exactly have a sign labeling it as such!

What a mess! Mountains are missing, boats are elusively hiding, and rumors abound. So what are we to make of this? How can we synthesize these different names, these different locations, and these different cultures, and find a common thread? The easiest and most often sought solution is to dismiss the peak as purely fictitious, viewing it as a symbol that refers to "the edge of the world."[5] This is convenient and easy, considering the peaks themselves are difficult — if not impossible — to locate, as we have already seen. Theodore Gaster, in his book *Myth, Legend, and Custom in the Old Testament*, notes that many cultures believed that a local mountain range was the end of the earth. Therefore, he argues, we should not view the mountains in the Flood myths as *actual* mountains. Instead, we should view the mountains as *symbolic* writing, indicating that the vessel came to rest beyond the reach of the known world, rather than at an actual given location. He gives as an example the Malayans, who viewed the Caucasus mountain range as "the hills of Qâf," a barrier protecting the earth from the "surrounding cosmic ocean."[6] Since there is no "surrounding cosmic ocean," he argues, we can view these mountains — and other fictitious mountains — as symbols. This makes sense . . . but only if we take the entire Flood story as a fable. If we take the Flood myth as history, and assume that the vessel was a *real* vessel, then we must also assume that it came to rest at a *real* location. Besides, as we shall see, the belief that the mountains were "the edge of the earth," so to speak, is not commonly held amongst *all* ancient peoples.

To many cultures, mountains — rather than representing the end of the world — merely served as barriers separating the peoples from more barbaric, less civilized cultures. The Hittites, for example, viewed the Caucasus Mountains as the dwelling place of the backward *Lullu* people, and the Greeks placed the Hyperboreans "in that general area."[7] This was not a fictional realm where monsters waited beyond the edge of the map to gobble up sailors and ships, but a real location with real inhabitants. In other words, as plausible as it is that the mountaintop location of the Flood vessel is merely symbolic, we cannot claim this is truth without being dogmatic, for mountain symbolism is *not* universal from culture to culture.

There may be a second theory, however, derived from our application of the diaspora and telephone mythology. The name probably refers to the highest peak visible *in the region in which this story was told*. Though its final location has been lost today, the peak was probably an actual mountain peak, easily identifiable to the original audience of the story. *If* the peak exists, then we can make two fairly safe assumptions. Either the peak named in a particular version of the story *is* the final resting place (and, hence, the source of the dispersion), or, as a *result* of the dispersion, has become a localized version of the actual resting place.

Parents wishing to instill the reality of the story to their children would gesture toward the local mountains and say, "That peak there is where the vessel landed." It is, simply, a way of making the story more personal and more tangible. To refer to a mountain "far away," or "further than the known world," would not suffice.

Through the diaspora, then, it is possible to understand given mountain names as personal and idealized versions of the original myth. This does not diminish the reality of an original resting place of the Flood vessel, but merely points out a possible explanation for the many varied locations given throughout the world.

For those who are unsatisfied with this explanation, there are a few potential connections between several versions. There is, for example, scant evidence to indicate that the Zagros mountain range, home of Mt. Nişir, was once considered part of the Ararat mountain range, tying the Gilgamesh epic to the *Torah*.[8] There is also a possible connection between the *Epic of Gilgamesh* and the *Mahābhārata*. Everest is called, in Hindi, Sagarmatha, and it is believed that the Zagros Mountains derived their name from the Sagarthian peoples, a name eerily similar to the Hindi name for Everest.[9] Understand, however, that both of these are merely conjectures and point to no real conclusion. The soundest reasoning for now, I believe, remains the idea that the different mountains named in the versions are all localized versions of the original resting place for the vessel. Other research may indicate something else later on, but for now, I'm comfortable with the "local legend" interpretation.

All four of these aspects — heroes, crew, cargo, and resting place — provide a clear example of telephone mythology in action. We see diverging details that fit within each culture's ideological framework, but we also see similarities that point to a common source. So again, while the independent evolution of local flood accounts is *possible*, it seems highly *improbable*.

The last detail we will look at in this book involves the appearance of animals at the end of the Flood. In some versions, the animals are sent out from the vessel as sort of a "litmus test": they are used to test whether the land is inhabitable again. In other versions, the animals are already external to the vessel and act as an "alert" that the land is dry again.

Endnotes

1. Charles Berlitz, *Lost Ship of Noah: In Search of the Ark at Ararat* (New York: G.P. Putnam's Sons, 1987), p. 33.
2. *Atharva Veda*, Book XIX, Hymn XXXIX, verse 8.
3. Pronounced: *jyoo-dē*.
4. Dr. Charles Willis, "Is This the Tomb of Noah?" www.ancient-worldfoundation.org. 2002.
5. Theodore Gaster, *Myth, Legend, and Custom in the Old Testament* (New York: Harper & Row, 1969), p. 128–129.
6. Ibid., p. 129.
7. Ibid.
8. Roy D. Holt, "Evidence for a Late Cainozoic Flood/post-Flood Boundary," *Creation Ex Nihilo Technical Journal*, vol. 10, no. 1 (1996): p. 147.
9. "Zagros Mountains," *Wikipedia*. http://en.wikipedia.org, 2006.

Chapter 9

THE FLOOD: ANIMALS AFTER THE DELUGE

Bored with the scenery, the man told an otter to dive down into the waters and see what he could find. The otter returned with a piece of earth. The man took the earth in his hand and breathed on it, and it began to grow. So he laid it on the water, kept it from sinking, and watched as it continued to grow. As it grew and grew, the man saw that it was becoming an island.
— The Flood according to the Montagnais, Hudson Bay

The last thread to which we will turn — very briefly — is the use of animals to determine the state of the earth after the Flood. The animals vary from version to version. There are birds in some versions, a fox in one, and a deer in another. And as much as the animals may vary, their uses vary, as well. In some, they are sent out of the vessel to *test for dry land*, while in others they are sent out onto *already dry land*. In a few versions, the animals are *outside* the vessel already. In these versions, they simply *announce* to the people inside the vessel that it is safe to come out and re-populate the earth. These are vast differences and seem, at first glance, irreconcilable. Is there a way to account for these changes? Let's take a look at the other versions in some more detail. For the full text of each of these versions, see appendix B.

In the Babylonian *Epic of Gilgamesh*, Utnapishtim first sends out a dove. The dove can find no place to land and so returns to the ark. Next, he sends a swallow, which also returns. Lastly, he sends a raven, and the raven, finding land, does not return. This has a *strong* resonance with the Genesis account. The main difference, of course, is that Noah sends out a *raven* first, and then he sends *two* doves. This idea of using a sort of "litmus test" for finding land is found farther east in Burma. In Burma, we're told the Chingpaw survivors use a series of cocks and needles to see when the earth is once again ready for habitation. They spend several days dropping the needles and cocks into the water, waiting for the cocks to crow and the needles to make a sound as they strike bottom. Once the cock crows, they figure dry land must be on the way. When they finally hear the needle strike the earth, they realize that the land is again dry and they can exit the vessel (though the precise connection between dry land and the rooster crowing is never explained).

The Hareskin Indians report that the hero of the Flood sent a muskrat into the water in order to see if he could touch the bottom. He failed, and after some time had passed, he tried again. He said that he could smell the earth, but he couldn't touch it. Lastly, the beaver tried, and when he came back, he was holding some mud in his hand. The hero took the mud, blew on it, and it turned into dry land. He then sent a fox onto the land. The man used the time it took the fox to run around the land as an indication of when the restoration of the earth was complete.

A similar idea is found in the Montagnais belief — from the Hudson Bay region of North America — except it is an otter that dives down and a reindeer that runs in a circuit around the land. Lastly, in Timor, the Rotti use animals as an appeasement to the water-god. After throwing a pig, a goat, a dog, a hen, and a cat into the waters, the god finally withdraws the flood and brings about dry land again by making special use of an osprey.

Obviously, some of the versions drew from each other. The Montagnais and Hareskin versions are clearly related to each other, both geographically and literarily. The stories are, in fact, so closely related that we could argue they developed together, borrowing from each other. The same could be said for the Hebrew and Babylonian versions. What we *should* be asking is whether or not we can find a deeper thread among *all* the versions. Can we find, in other words, a connection between, say, the North American versions and the version from Timor? Or can we perhaps find a parallel between the Babylonian version and the Chinese tales? *Do these threads exist?*

There actually appear to be *two* strong threads here. The first thread involves the use of birds. We find this thread spreading from Mesopotamia — the Babylonian and Hebrew versions — and east. The Asian versions almost all have this thread. In China, for example, the Bhanars tell of a brother and sister that escape the Deluge by hiding in a box. They know when the waters have receded because a rooster, sent by their ancestors, crows. The thread changes, of course, in that the rooster comes from outside of the vessel rather than from within, but this common theme of a bird *alerting* the crew to the presence of dry land is quite strong.

The second thread involves the use of a "litmus test" — the sending out of animals to "test" for dry land. In the Babylonian and Hebrew versions, the heroes use birds. In the West (North and South America), however, completely different animals are used, but they *serve the same function*.

The migration of these threads is unusual and impressive, and I believe we can explain this phenomenon with three *possible* scenarios. The first scenario is that the central version — either the *actual event itself* or a *very near relative* — is one of the Middle-Eastern versions. From there, then, the diaspora carried the tale until the different stories had evolved into the extreme versions found at either end of the spectrum.

If, for example, the use of birds, or the "bird" thread, were followed from the Mesopotamian versions, we would see something to this effect: first, birds are being used to test for dry land (Hebrew/Babylonian); second, a cock, specifically, is being used to test for dry land (Burmese); third, a cock crows from *outside* the vessel sometime after the Flood, alerting the people to the fact that the land is dry (Chinese). If we were to follow the "litmus test" thread, it might have developed something like this: first, the hero used birds to test for dry land (Hebrew/Babylonian); second, the hero used a muskrat and an otter to test for dry land, then, once the land appeared, used a fox to determine when the land was habitable (Hareskin); third, the hero used *just* an otter to test for land, then used a more regionally appropriate *reindeer* to determine when the land was habitable (Montagnais). This is only one possible scenario.

The next scenario involves the source version being somewhere in the Americas. The story would have then spread north and west into Russia and Asia. This spread would have evolved from a version where the hero used different kinds of animals to test the waters, to a version where the hero used different *birds* to test the waters (Genesis and Gilgamesh). Eventually, the idea of "testing" the waters disappears, but the *bird thread remains* as the story spreads south into Asia.

The last scenario would, in truth, simply reverse the order. We might start with birds "announcing" or (in the Rotti version) "creating" dry land. That may evolve into a story where the bird is used to "test" the dry land, which may then evolve into other assorted animals "testing" the land.

The threads are common enough to be skeptical about the "independent evolution" of each version. However, the changes can easily be traced through telephone mythology. Remember, I am not necessarily commenting on how the story *definitely* changed, but merely how the story *possibly* changed.

In several brief glimpses, we have looked at the hero, the cargo, the crew, the final resting places of the vessels, and the use of animals after the Flood. Each version is remarkably similar to the other versions. More telling, however, is that each version has a *direct parallel* to another version. That parallel often occurs between versions that are separated by vast geographic distances, as is the case with the crew members in the Sanskrit and Hebrew text. If each of these versions was invented independently of each other, can we explain these parallels? We cannot do so easily. However, if each version was passed down from another version — and, ultimately, from the true version — would we be able to explain those parallels? We could do *that* quite easily.

Still, the argument is that the flood legends all tell of local disasters. To be certain, many of them *may be* local flood legends. But can we safely take that stance with *every* version? The next chapter explores that.

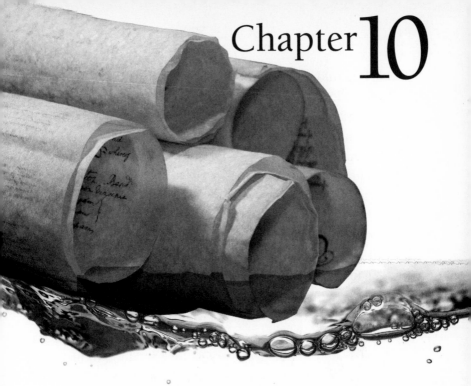

Chapter 10

LOCAL VERSUS GLOBAL

The Earth was shaken to its foundations. The sky sank lower toward the north. The sun, moon, and stars changed their motions. The Earth fell to pieces and the waters in its bosom rushed upward with violence and overflowed the Earth. Man had rebelled against the high gods, and the system of the Universe was in disorder. The planets altered their courses, and the grand harmony of the Universe and nature was disturbed.
— The *Ch'in-ting-ku-chin-t'su-shu-shi-ch'eng*, China

The last element I wish to discuss is more a critique of the "local flood" arguments, using the literature as a guide. The very language of the myths themselves implies that the floods were not local but did in fact cover the earth. In the

Torah, God informs Noah that He is about to "destroy all flesh under the sky in which there is breath of life," and that, when the waters come, they swell "fifteen cubits higher" than the "highest mountain." Assuming Everest was at its current height, the water in the *Torah* would have had a depth of 29,050 feet. In the *Mahābhārata*, Brahma (the Fish) informs Manu that the "dissolution of all moving and unmoving things of earth is near," and that, when the Deluge came, "all was sea." These myths are full of interesting contradictions, if we are to believe they refer only to local floods.

The first contradiction is the fact that water seeks its own level, and would therefore not cover mountains if only a valley were filled. To put it another way, if the water were high enough to cover the tallest mountains, then we would expect — indeed, it would be *necessary* — for the Flood to be more than local. Water cannot cover the highest point on earth in one section, and then drop below that level in another section. That is impossible. It would, in fact, be necessary for the Flood to reach a global scale. We read in the Sanskrit text that only Manu, the Ṛsis, and the Fish can be seen in the "disordered world," indicating that everything else was covered with water. The Kariña account reports, "You could no longer see the tops of even the tallest trees." Had the Flood, in each of these cultures, been merely local, there would have been hills, acting like the edge of a soup bowl, visible just above the waterline and holding the water in place.

The second contradiction in the stories — if we are to believe they refer to local floods — is that, had the Flood only been local and mountains and trees exposed, then birds, animals, and even people could have moved to safer areas. Logically following that, it would have been unnecessary to either save the creatures (as in Genesis) or re-create them (as in the *Mahābhārata*); these actions would be necessary only if the destruction of life were *total*.

Lastly, in terms of linguistic patterns, in the Hebrew, the word used for Flood is *mabbool* (or, also, *mabbul*), whose Greek equivalent would be *kataklusmos*. This is where we get our word "cataclysm." Neither *mabbool* nor *kataklusmos* is typical for "flood," but imply a more catastrophic, earth-altering event. Some models picture the water being hot, even boiling, as it breaks from the earth's crust. Others have a canopy of water collapsing onto the earth in a sudden, violent downpour (though the so-called canopy model is no longer considered a credible theory). Either event would have been more than a mere flood. Both events describe tremendous catastrophes.

This idea of a catastrophic, earth-altering event is not just found in Genesis. The Icelandic epic, Edda, describes the coming of the Flood this way:

> Mountains dash together . . .
> And heaven is split in two.
> The sun grows dead —
> The earth sinks into the sea.
> The bright stars vanish.
> Fires rage and raise their flames
> As high as heaven.[1]

A tribe of people from Assam, known as the Lushais, tell that prior to the Flood, the earth was one flat plain, but that the water, when it came, carved out the valleys and mountains that we see today. Gaster tells of a New Zealand people group that landed on the earth after the Flood and discovered, to their dismay, that "all was changed." He retells the story in this way: "The earth was cracked and fissured in some places, and in others it had been turned upside down and confounded by reason of the Flood. And not one soul was left alive in the world."[2] In the Imperial Chinese work *Ch'in-ting-ku-chin-t'su-shu-shi-ch'eng*, the Deluge is described as "[shaking] the Earth

. . . to its foundations," and that "the sky sank lower toward the north" while "the Earth fell to pieces and the water in its bosom rushed upward with violence."[3]

In the *Mahābhārata*, the language *distinctly* states "all ends in *violent* water" (emphasis added). To further drive this home, the Fish reminds Manu that all that is "mobile" and "immobile" will be destroyed — a literary technique that implies that *everything on earth* will perish in this deluge. Brahma does not indicate that all of India will perish, nor does the tale indicate that Manu must merely re-create a village. Rather, Brahma tells Manu that everything on *earth* will be destroyed, both the animate and inanimate, and Manu must re-create *everything* after the Flood. Furthermore, in the Hebrew text, the survivors remained in the ark for 53 weeks, and in the Sanskrit, it was several years (imagine spending *years* on a boat, with nothing to eat but seeds!). In a local flood, dry land would have been just beyond the horizon, easily reached in a small amount of time. Because many mythologists and historians have recognized this fact — that the cultures who wrote the stories clearly saw the catastrophes as global floods — the world of academia has tended to side with a newer interpretation of the myths. They argue that the cultures were simply unable to tell the difference between "local" and "global," interpreting what amounts to merely a local flood as something far more destructive.

A recent book by William Ryan and Walter Pitman[4] suggests that the Flood can *easily* be identified as a local, but still catastrophic, flood. The authors refer to the clear presence of ruins at the bottom of the Black Sea. The area shows evidence of once being a dry valley, which was later flooded when rising sea levels poured through the Bosporous Strait, creating what is now the Black Sea. They believe that groups of families living on the far side of the valley were able to see the water levels rising and escape in rapidly constructed boats. Ryan and Pitman theorize that *this* event was the basis for the global flood stories of Genesis and the Gilgamesh epic. However, their hypothesis fails to explain how cultures from *other parts of the world* also came up with similar stories. In addition, it fails to explain the very language of the stories, which, as we have seen, does *not* indicate the Flood was merely local. On an interesting side note, there is a Turkish legend that Alexander the Great, out of anger at a Turkish queen, dug a trench into the Bosporous, which then flooded, creating the strait that now exists there (perhaps, then, Ryan's and Pitman's very *interpretation* of the formation of the Black Sea needs some revisiting, as well). Even so, the argument still persists that these various cultures around the world simply did not know the difference between "local" and "global."

Few people who delve into this realm of Deluge mythology even note differences between local and global flood myths. For example, Gaster, in his chapter on the Deluge, lists several cultures that have what he refers to as "Global Deluge Myths," but which clearly refer to *local* floods.

An old legend in Washington State, popular among the Native American tribes that used to settle there, tells of an old man who escaped a flood in "all the country" by seeking refuge in the mountains.[5] Nowhere does the story suggest that the Flood was global but gives every indication that it was a local event. In Tierra del Fuego, they claim that all but a single high mountain was submerged, and the survivors were those who had made it to the mountain.[6] These would be clear examples of *local* flood stories, because higher ground was available. The *global* versions indicate just the opposite: that *nothing* remained until the waters receded.

Furthermore, many ancient cultures that have a global deluge myth also carry myths of local floods within their literature. In a later passage in Genesis we read: "Now, when King Amraphel of Shinar, King Arioch of Ellasar, King

Chedorlaomer of Elam, and King Tidal of Goiim made war on King Bera of Sodom, King Birsha of Gomorrah, King Shinab of Admah, King Shemeber of Zeboiim, and the King of Bela, which is Zoar, all the latter joined forces *at the Valley of Siddim, now the Dead Sea.*"[7] At the time of the composition of the text, the author had already written about the Flood but was now telling of a valley that had been flooded so completely that it had acquired a new name: "Dead Sea." Would Moses have recognized the difference between *local* and *global*? Would he have known that a flood that covered the earth would be more catastrophic than a flood that filled a valley? He certainly wrote about them differently. Without being dogmatic, the compiler of Genesis truly appeared to know the difference between the two types of floods.

The *Mahābhārata* tells, in an earlier chapter of Book III, how Krishna "will sink Dvārakā in the ocean."[8] Dvārakā was — and still is — a city in Western India. About 20 years ago, however, the ruins of an ancient city were discovered underwater a few miles off the coast of present-day Dvārakā, indicating that the city had, in fact, been flooded. Most importantly, however, the text states that the city, *and only the city*, would be flooded. Again, inclusion of a clear story of a local flood within the text makes it quite obvious that the culture could tell the difference between a local flood and a global deluge.

The Egyptians, who thrived on the annual flooding of the Nile, also have a global deluge story. The Greeks, whose hero Deucalion survives a global deluge, also tell of the "Flood of Arcadia," which drove King Dardanos and his subjects out of the lowlands for many years, forcing them to take refuge in the mountains.[9] Again, we see two different stories: in one version, building a ship for survival is *necessary*; in the other, escape to higher ground is possible.

When looking at the literature itself, can we honestly say that the stories refer to local floods? Not without performing great feats of mental gymnastics. Plus, to assume these cultures could not tell a difference between global and local is to assume *vast ignorance* on their part. We can hardly look back on the ancient Greeks, or the Babylonians, or the Egyptians, and claim that they were ignorant cultures. And yet from *almost every major culture* — even the "highly advanced" ones, such as the Greeks, Babylonians, and Egyptians — we find a story of a global deluge.

While scholars insist that, throughout the world, cultures evolved separately and formed their own unique versions of a global deluge based on flooding rivers, tidal waves, and so forth, there is a large body of evidence, within most cultural literature, to suggest otherwise. Common sense tells us that the literature itself points to a global flood. If, as many believe, these deluge myths are products of independent imaginations, how *do* we account for the eerily similar details amongst the versions?

We cannot.

On the other hand, if these various myths all have a common source, can we account for the differences?

We certainly can.

The differences in the myths arise, not because each myth was "invented" independently of other myths, but because the stories all share a common origin and have been filtered through an international, multicultural game of "telephone." The similarities arise because the stories all share a common origin. From a literary standpoint, we cannot claim anything less.

Endnotes
1. Charles Berlitz, *Lost Ship of Noah: In Search of the Ark at Ararat* (New York: G.P. Putnam's Sons, 1987), p. 121.
2. Theodore Gaster, *Myth, Legend, and Custom in the Old Testament* (New York: Harper and Row Publishers, 1969)), p. 111.
3. Berlitz, *Lost Ship of Noah*, p. 126.

4. William Ryan and Walter Pitman, *Noah's Flood: The New Scientific Discoveries About the Event That Changed History* (New York: Simon & Schuster, 1998).

5. Gaster, *Myth, Legend, and Custom in the Old Testament,* p. 119.

6. Ibid., p. 128.

7. Gen. 14:1–3, *Tanakh* (Jewish Publications Society, Philadelphia, PA), emphasis added.

8. *Mahābhārata,* III:12/35.

9. Gaster, *Myth, Legend, and Custom in the Old Testament,* p. 84–85, 89.

Chapter 11

TRUTH OR OPINION?

This is how you are to build it: The ark is to be 450 feet long, 75 feet wide and 45 feet high (Gen. 6:15).

We've looked at the literature in great detail. We've looked at different versions. We've seen that the numerous versions all have enough differences to make them unique to their cultures. We've also seen enough similarities to be wary of the "independent evolution" theory of the stories. We've seen how a new method of interpretation — telephone mythology — can explain many of the similarities *and* differences.

Still, is theory enough? We can find parallels in the beliefs of many ancient cultures, but does that necessarily mean that the beliefs are accurate? For example, in Greek mythology, the god Zeus uses lightning bolts as weapons, hurling them to earth at will. In Hindu mythology, it is the sky-god Indra who uses lightning as a weapon. Here we have a *very strong* parallel, but does the parallel guarantee accuracy? Not in this particular case, because we know how lightning forms.

Could all of this theorizing that we have done be for naught, then? Can we find, not a "theoretical flood," but the actual, historically accurate version? Is there an accurate version, or is it, as some say, simply a matter of opinion? Can *all* opinions be right, or is there such a thing as truth?

Quid est Veritas?

Let's start there. First and foremost, we need to differentiate between fact and opinion. Opinions are subjective. That means that there is no real way to measure or confirm a statement of opinion, and, therefore, contradictory opinions can both be valid. For example, if you were to claim, "Apples taste better than oranges," I may agree with you — or I may disagree with you — but you are neither right nor wrong. There is no way to measure "taste," because it is a matter of opinion; there is not one universal truth about the taste of apples versus the taste of oranges. Therefore, the statement "apples taste better than oranges" is a subjective statement, because it is *subject* to your opinion.

An objective statement deals with a measurable and viable truth (or a measurable and viable *object*). We can usually evaluate an objective statement with quantitative data. If I said that a six-foot-tall person is taller than a five-foot-tall person, that would be an objective statement. It is not a matter of opinion but can be either verified or falsified because we can measure the difference between six feet and five feet and see that, in fact, my statement is *true*.

Likewise, if I said, "Italy is in the United States," we can test the accuracy of that statement. Italy, as it turns out, is on a map, as is the United States. All one would have to do is look at a map of the world to determine whether my statement were true or not. Because Italy is in Europe and not the United Sates, my assertion cannot be called an opinion because it is *verifiably false*. Neither of these are statements of opinions, but statements of fact. And because fact involves existing truth, it is either right or wrong. My first statement about the person's height was correct. My second statement about Italy was *incorrect*.

Opinions, because they are not measurable, can contradict each other and still be viable opinions. Facts cannot be both contradictory and still accurate. Italy cannot be in both Europe and the United States. Opinions deal with *personal taste*. Facts deal with *historicity*. Opinions can change, but no matter how strongly I may feel about them, they can never be "true." The moment they become "true" or "false" they become *facts*. Statements of fact, on the other hand, are either true or false, regardless of how seriously I may feel about the subject. I may feel, very deeply, that Italy is in the United States, but I would be very deeply wrong.

What happens if we are dealing with a truth that cannot be measured? What happens when we are dealing with a truth about a historical event from the past, an event that we cannot witness today? Can it still be fact? Yes, because fact is fact, regardless of how we feel about it. A global flood either happened, or it did not. It is either a historical fact or a fictional blunder and *cannot be* a matter of opinion. Likewise, if the Flood happened, it *must have happened a certain way*. The "true" way is not a matter of opinion. For example, the rain either lasted for 40 days and nights, or it didn't. That means that either the Genesis version is accurate, or it is not. Since we have every reason to believe in the Flood — from all of the numerous recorded accounts — and since different versions of the Flood contradict each other, they cannot all be accurate. We cannot assert that the Flood vessel had only two people on board and at the same time claim that it had eight people on board. It *did* have a certain number on board, but we cannot claim that every version is accurate on this point. *At least one of them must be correct, and all others wrong.* So it seems as if we now have the difficult task of determining, if possible, which version is accurate.

Can we do that? After all, we weren't there when it happened, so how do *we* know which version is accurate? In this case, because the event is no longer completely verifiable, we have to use a mixture of what we *do* know with some pure, good old-fashioned logic. In other words, we may not be able to *prove* one version over another, but we can *support* one version over another *beyond reasonable doubt*. We do know that archaeology and anthropology have revealed some interesting evidence for the beginnings of civilization, so the first place to start may be looking at the general, historical flow of civilization.

If the diaspora happened, then we would expect to find the center of it — the "Tower of Babel," so to speak — at the birthplace of civilization. The so-called Cradle of Civilization has long been considered to be in the ancient Mesopotamian region, or the modern-day Middle East.[1] While most anthropologists claim that this is where civilization started, I submit that, during a global deluge, all prior evidence of civilization would more than likely have been erased. Therefore, what we consider to be the place where civilization *started* may in fact be the place where civilization *restarted*; in other words, where the survivors of the Deluge began to rebuild. If civilization restarted there after the Deluge, there is a *very good* chance that the Middle East is, therefore, the source of the diaspora. So a good starting point would probably involve a closer look at the Mesopotamian versions of the Flood.

The Cradle of Civilization

The belief has long been held that the Babylonian *Epic of Gilgamesh* is the earliest version of the Flood myth known, and that it more than likely influenced the writing of the Genesis version. So let's start there. Could the *Epic of Gilgamesh* be the original version of the Flood?

It certainly is *older* than the Genesis version. The original cuneiform tablets, translated by George Smith in the early 1870s, are believed to be *at least* 3,700 years old (compared to Moses' manuscripts, written about 3,400 years ago). While it has been argued that Moses merely compiled older, oral legends for his work, the *hard data* remains that the Gilgamesh tablets are in fact more ancient than the Hebrew manuscripts. However, there are a few reasons to suspect that the Babylonian version was *passed down* to the Babylonians from an original — probably oral — source.

The first is the immortality of the hero and his wife. Now, I am not suggesting that divine beings should not be able to bestow immortality on people . . . not at all. It seems realistic that they should be able to bend the laws of nature. However, if these people *were* truly immortal, then we would expect to see them around today. The simple fact *is* that we do not. I have not been able to locate any Utnapishtim who survived the global Deluge, nor have I seen *any record* of this hero alive today. There simply seems to be no Utnapishtim. Right there, we have a *serious historical contradiction* in the literature. *Is* it possible that Utnapishtim is still alive somewhere in the Middle East, hiding out with his wife? Because of the severe apparent lack of evidence of the Flood hero today, I can say, with sureness and confidence, that the Babylonian version is inaccurate on this point.

The second problem that arises in the text is the *size* of the craft. The vessel appears to be a perfect cube, measuring 30 cubits on each side. Because a cubit is roughly 1'4", that means the vessel has only some 64,000 cubic feet of space. Utnapishtim is instructed to bring a pair of every living thing, along with his family and provisions. That, simply, is not enough space, particularly when contrasted with the Genesis vessel's nearly 1.1 million cubic feet of space.

Genesis tells us that the ark was 300 cubits long, 50 cubits wide, and 30 cubits tall. That converts to roughly 400 feet by 60 feet by 40 feet. Noah is instructed to build three levels, giving him a total of 79,200 square feet of usable floor space. Each level would have been some 13 feet tall, allowing plenty of room for stacking provisions, cages, and so forth. Even if Utnapishtim's vessel also had three levels, that would have allowed only 4,800 square feet of usable floor space, or about five percent of the space in the Genesis vessel.

John Woodmorappe, author of *Noah's Ark: A Feasibility Study*, actually breaks down the various details of the story — including the number of animals possibly on the ark (he estimates approximately 16,000 animals on board[2]) — looking at it from a purely statistical standpoint. His argument, though it has several critics, is extremely thorough and well researched. Without being able to prove the Genesis account (he was not there, either), he goes a long way toward lending it credibility.

Right here, we find two severe problems with the Gilgamesh version. The first is the apparent historical inaccuracy involving the hero. The second is nothing more than a feasibility problem. What about the Genesis version, though? Other than cargo and size, can the Genesis version be trusted? Well, that version seems the more logical of the two, for many reasons.

First, the size of the vessel in reference to the cargo is more reasonable. Secondly, the fact that Noah is treated, from beginning to end, as a human — without gaining "immortality" — seems more in line with what we observe today. Lastly, Noah's crew members are identified and their lineage given — a lineage that can be traced, historically, to various parts of the world.

Placed next to the Genesis version, the Babylonian version *sounds* more like a fairytale. This is not to say that the Babylonians *made up* their version. Not at all; the two versions are far too alike to be independently invented. The changes and distortions we see are, most likely, the result of the dispersion. Telephone mythology shrank the size of the vessel, turned the monotheistic Noah into a polytheistic Utnapishtim, and the rainbow — a natural occurrence after rain — became the jeweled necklace of Ishtar.

If the dispersion happened in the Mesopotamian region, then we can expect one of these two versions to be the original, "source" version. Comparing the two stories, basing our judgments solely on the text, the Genesis version seems to be the more logical of the two. I consider the Hebrew version to be the source of the Flood legends from around the globe.

Now I know what you're thinking. Can I just easily dismiss the other two versions that we've looked at? Why can the Sanskrit version not be the accurate version? What about the Kariña version? How can I summarily — some would say whimsically — toss the other versions aside? Is this a sneaky, underhanded, creationist trick? Not at all. Let's look at the three versions and really analyze them for feasibility.

The Hero

First, from the point of view of the hero, I would very much hesitate to accept the Sanskrit version. Remember, the point of the hero is that he is a virtuous, upright (at least in heart) person who obeys his god. From a character-trait-driven perspective, this is not difficult to imagine. We have all known at least one good person in our lives. My father is one of them: he is a kind, gentle man who is generous with both his time and money. However, from a realistic and feasible standpoint, I have reservations in regards to the Hindu version.

No matter how pious a person may be, I cannot envision him or her standing on one foot, soaking wet, for a thousand years. Even if the text were speaking in hyperbole — which it gives no indication of doing — interpreting it another way is simply impossible; there is no room for another translation without seriously disregarding the existing text. On the other hand, if we were to look at the Kariña and Hebrew versions, those heroes are more believable. The Kariña survivors recognize Kaputano's supremacy and obey him . . . they heed his warning. Likewise, Noah is "righteous" and "blameless before God," and, therefore, heeds God's warning. *If* a person were communing with God, and *if* God were to give a warning regarding a flood, then we can reasonably expect the person to react accordingly. However, *if* a man were pious, and *if* a man were an ascetic, can we reasonably expect him to stand on one foot, soaking wet, for a thousand years? Not really. From a very physical perspective, no matter *how* pious a person is, his foot cannot support him for a thousand years; it is virtually impossible.

Please understand that I am not trying to make light of the Hindu version. However, from a purely practical standpoint, if I were forced to eliminate the accuracy of one version based solely on the hero's characteristics, it would be the *Mahābhārata*. There are, however, other reasons I would dismiss this version, as well.

Crew and Cargo

In looking at the crew and cargo, there are several fac-
tors to consider, first of which would be the number of crew
members. The simple fact that all three primary versions tell
us that eight people were on the vessel is a *strong* argument
for the historical validity of a deluge. But which eight people
were they? Were they "four couples," a family, or the hero and
his seven wise sages? From a textual standpoint, I don't think
it much matters, because each version is *contextually feasible*.
That is to say, eight people on board are a reasonable number,
and, within each story, the crew members make sense.

For example, within the framework of the Genesis version, where God chooses one man to build his ark, we could
reasonably expect God to also choose that man's family as
the crew. Within the Kariña version, Kaputano arrives on
earth and addresses *everyone*, thus giving *everyone* a chance
to respond. In this case, we could reasonably expect that the
four different couples who do speak up would not necessarily be related. Within the framework of the Fish Story, where
Manu re-creates everything, we simply do not need a group
of couples that can procreate, and therefore the Ṛsis would
suffice.

Nonetheless, I have a simple reservation about accepting
the presence of the Ṛsis: I am unsure of their validity. Please
do not misunderstand me: I have no doubt that at some point
in time the Ṛsis actually existed. Remember, though, that
within the Sanskrit literature, the Ṛsis usually act as stock
characters, appearing in a variety of places and at different
points in history. They show up, as I've said before, whenever
holy characters are needed. This indicates one of several possible scenarios.

First, the seven Ṛsis are immortal. I find this highly unlikely. Without discounting it completely, we simply have no

evidence that the immortal characters in ancient literature are still alive today (which is what we would expect from immortal characters). Again, the Gilgamesh epic tells us that the heroes of the Flood, Utnapishtim and his wife, were blessed with immortality. If my understanding of immortality is correct, then we would expect Utnapishtim and his wife to still be alive today. They are not, however, at least not to my knowledge. Likewise, the Seven Ṛsis, as a group of people, are not alive and well in India today. Again, without being willing to completely dismiss the literature, we can safely regard this scenario as *highly unlikely*.

The second scenario is that there has been more than one group of Ṛsis throughout history, and the Ṛsis in the vessel with Manu are different from the Ṛsis that appear in later (or earlier) literature. This one is actually possible. The Ṛsis may not refer to specific *people*, but, instead, a specific *group* or *class* of people. "Ṛsi" is often translated as "sage," and could be a reference to their social status. This is hinted at in the *Rig Veda*, Book X, where it is said that, in reference to the original Ṛsis, newer ones have "taken up the reins like chariot drivers," indicating that these "sages" are a type of club or elite group that would train and groom successors. However, as mentioned above, the group of Seven Ṛsis, as an organization, is no longer around, so the precise interpretation of the term is still up in the air. Individual sages can be found throughout India and other parts of Southeastern Asia, but a formal group of them no longer exists. So while I accept this scenario, I do so with reservations.

Lastly, though, the presence of the sages in the Fish Story may indicate that the seven Ṛsis *represent* the seven people who were *actually on the vessel with the hero*. There were, at some point, seven other crew members with the hero. What I believe happened is that the identity of those seven was, ultimately, lost, and the original passengers were replaced with the culturally appropriate Ṛsis. I find this scenario the *most* likely out of the three. If the source of the diaspora was the Middle East, then this particular thread was kept as the story passed on, but the details became lost, adapting themselves to the changing cultures. Couple this hypothesis with the already questionable account of the hero, and I have some severe reservations accepting the Sanskrit version as accurate. On the other hand, there *is* the cargo to consider.

The cargo is truly and undeniably feasible if the Sanskrit version is accurate. Manu and the seven Ṛsis brought aboard seeds. There were no animals with which to contend, there was no waste from the animals, no elephant trumpeting, no geese squawking, no dogs barking, no cats giving the humans attitude. . . . The Hindu version is truly feasible from a cargo perspective. In the other two versions, each of which contains both seeds and animals, we potentially run into an entire host of problems. Among the problems are care and feeding, waste disposal, and, most of all, storage. To tackle the storage problem, we would need to examine the size of the vessels.

In the Kariña myth, we are not told how large the vessel was. All we are told was that it was a canoe, large enough to hold everyone and everything on board. From a feasibility study, then, there is little we can do in order to gain answers. The Hebrew version, on the other hand, gives us actual dimensions of the vessel but fails to tell us how many animals are on board. If Woodmorappe's estimates are correct, however, 1.1 million cubic feet of space is plenty of room for 16,000 animals, plus feed and other supplies. More than one million cubic feet of space is equivalent to more than 500 railway stock cars, and with 16,000 animals on board, would leave approximately 69 cubic feet of space *per animal*. Obviously, a pair of ravens would not need 138 cubic feet of space, nor would a pair of rabbits. Because of the extra space afforded by the smaller animals, there is *potentially* enough room for the larger animals, as well as feed and other supplies.

So which cargo manifest is most likely? The Sanskrit version is, by far, the most practical. However, as we have seen, when it comes to its details regarding both the hero and the crew, a certain amount of skepticism will always surround this version, at least in my mind. The Hebrew version would seem — and usually is taken as — completely unreliable, but Woodmorappe's work has shed immense light on the technical problems surrounding the *Torah* version. The Kariña version, on the other hand, simply does not give us enough information. It may be *completely* feasible, but it also may not. Does the term "canoe" mean a literal canoe, or is that simply the Kariña word for any seagoing vessel? We do not know. All we are told is that it is large. As such, it would be dogmatic either way to push for or against the Kariña version.

Animals and the Flood

Is it feasible to send animals out of a ship to test for dry land? Sure. Why not?

What about the changes in the animals used? What about the changes in *how* the animals are used? And how can we tell, if at all, which version is accurate? I submit that a *clear and concise progressive chain exists in these stories*.

If we take the Middle East as the source of the diaspora, then we see two very strong threads emerge. At the center of the diaspora is the idea that the hero of the Flood used birds as an indication — or "litmus test" — of the habitability of the earth. Spreading west into North America, the story lost the "bird" thread but kept the "litmus test" thread. As it spread east into Asia, it lost the "litmus" thread but retained the "bird" thread.

Understand, I am not claiming this *is* how it happened, only that this is how it *could have* happened. It is fairly easy to surmise that the birds of the Middle-Eastern versions became the cocks of the Asian versions. The changes were probably slower, but they are, more than likely, there. I suspect that the transition was from the various birds to the single cock crowing outside the vessel. This would have then evolved into the version where the cocks were thrown from the vessel, along with the needles. However, having said that, we could, in fact, reverse those two.

The last twig on this branch is the Rotti version, from Timor. While the survivors initially use animals to placate the sea-god, there is one interesting detail: after the sea-god agrees to the animal sacrifices, it is the osprey that comes forth and actually *creates* the dry land. What is vital here is that the bird appears, *even though the sea-god promises to withdraw the waters, thus rendering the bird unnecessary*. Why is this vital? Common threads. Assuming the inhabitants of Timor arrived from the northern Asian mainland, the story would change, of course, but it would retain the common thread found in the other versions.

The left branch is what I call the "animal branch." It extends through North America and into South America. I suspect that the three birds turned into the three animals diving into the water: the muskrat (twice), then the beaver. Interestingly enough, there is the appearance of the fox, whose sole purpose is to alert them as to when the land is ready. The Montagnais literature eliminates the three diving animals and consolidates them into one venture: the otter's dive. The fox remains but transforms into the more regionally accurate reindeer.

The wild card in all of this is the Rotti version, out of Timor. Timor, located in Indonesia, should have only the bird thread, without the litmus test thread. However, it has *both*. This could mean one of two things. First, the Timor version spread, not from Asia, but from North America. However, since that seems rather unlikely, I tend to lean more toward the second possibility, which is that, while the story, overall, lost the "litmus" thread, some cultures retained that detail, and the Rotti version is the version we have today that contains both of the threads.

The Final Landing of the Vessel

As far as the final resting place of the vessel goes, if the water truly covered the top of the highest mountain, then the ship coming to rest on a mountain is quite feasible. However, in the Sanskrit version, we have a mountain that *cannot be located* — in fact, cannot even be identified with *any* existing mountains. In the Hebrew version, we have a mountain range that is still known today. Which seems more accurate? It should be noted that, in the Kariña version, the vessel came to rest in the plains. While this is a perfectly *reasonable* idea, it simply has the weight of every other version against it, for nearly every other flood myth in the world has the vessel landing on a mountain.

So right here, in just a few quick glances, we have seen that, yes, the details are feasible, but more importantly, they are much more likely to have developed from the Genesis version. Have I proven the Genesis version? No, but if we take the idea that civilization started in Mesopotamia (or, more likely, restarted there), and we compare the different Mesopotamian versions to each other, we can, *within reason*, believe the Genesis version is accurate.

Nevertheless, this works best when we can demonstrate that the other versions emanated *from* the Genesis version. If the core of the event is in the present-day Middle East, then we should see the "watering-down" of the story increase as cultures spread outward from the area. The next chapter looks at that.

Endnotes
1. Norman F. Cantor, ed., *Ancient Civilization: 4000 B.C.–400 A.D.,* Daniel, Glyn, "The Advent of Civilization" (New York: Thomas Y. Crowell Company, 1972), p. 4.
2. John Woodmorappe, *Noah's Ark: A Feasibility Study* (Santee, CA: Institute for Creation Research, 1996), p. 10.

Chapter 12

THE ORIGIN OF THE STORY

*You are aware of Shurrupak. It is a city on
the banks of the Euphrates. The city is old . . .
ancient . . . and, once upon a time, the very
gods lived in it. They reveled in its majesty.*
— The Flood according to the Babylonians

Most anthropologists and historians believe that the
spread of civilization unfolded as follows: humans, first
moving out of Africa, began to develop language, cities, and
so forth in Mesopotamia, or the modern-day Middle East.
This region is often called the "Cradle of Civilization." The
people then began to spread out, some moving north and
west into Europe, others spreading into Asia. Once in Asia, it
is believed they spread north throughout Russia, and south

into Southeast Asia, where they crossed the ocean and inhab-
ited the islands of Indonesia. Eventually, they began to reach
Australia. The ones that spread north into Russia eventually
made their way across the Bering Strait, migrating south into
the Americas.[1] In this chapter, we're going to follow this basic
idea, using the literature to see if, in fact, telephone mythology becomes visibly manifest.

The Early Versions

Coming from Mesopotamia and moving northwest would
bring us to the Greek myth of Deucalion and Pyrrah. In the
Greek version, the parallels to the Middle Eastern versions
are *remarkable*. The hero is told to build a box of wood (similar to the Hebrew version, but much more closely related to
the Babylonian version, as most Greek artwork depicts the
vessel as being a cube). What we have, then, is this idea of a
box (as opposed to a boat) that is rectangular in shape, but,
as the story is passed down to other generations, becomes
more of a cube.

Where in most versions the vessel is a raft or ship, this
very original idea of a box is interesting. However, while that
thread remains in *place*, it does not necessarily remain *intact*,
for the size of the vessel appears to shrink. We have a rectangular vessel a little more than one million cubic feet in volume, which then changes to a cube-like vessel only 64,000
cubic feet in volume. That vessel then appears to be "watered
down" (no pun intended) to a cube that is large enough to
accommodate just the hero and his wife, without the added
room needed for other crew members.

Secondly, we see the number of crew members on the
ship decrease. In the Genesis version, the eight passengers
on board are identified for us. In the Gilgamesh Epic, we are
merely told that it is Utnapishtim, his wife, and his "family."
How many were in his family? The text does not say. All we

have is the remaining portion of that particular detail, an obscure and unidentified number. In the Greek version, however,
even that portion of the crew is lost, and it is only Deucalion
and Pyrrah who board the vessel.

What we have, then, moving from the Torah, through the
Epic of Gilgamesh, and into Greece, are two points of interest:
vessel shape and reduction of crew. These two changes are
an immediate, observable evolution and stem, no doubt, from
the disapora and this idea of telephone mythology.

From the Middle East, it is generally agreed that civilization spread east, into India. India, of course, is home to the
Sanskrit Fish Myth. As we have seen, the parallels are extremely strong: warning from the Creator, building of a ship,
stocking of seeds, virtues of the hero, and number of crew
members on board. We have already looked at how the differences are indicative of the culture: instead of the hero and
his seven family members, it is the hero and the seven Ṛsis.
Because Manu and the Ṛsis cannot propagate life, Manu — by
his virtue and piety — must therefore re-create life.

The Middle Versions

From India, it is said that people groups split into two
movements, some going south into Southeast Asia, eventually
crossing the ocean into Indonesia and Australia. The second
group, it is agreed, moved northeast, eventually crossing the
Bering Strait and entering into North America. We'll follow
the southern branch first.

This brings us to the Burmese myth. Here, we still have
the strong re-creation thread passed on from the Sanskrit
version, but we also find the "bird" and "litmus" threads reappearing. Rather than reappearing, though, what has probably happened is that the threads were never "lost," so to
speak, but were passed on through a different culture than
the one that created the *Mahābhārata*. In essence, I believe

this thread, though not found in the Fish Myth, was still moving and evolving throughout other different cultures.

The other thread still present is the supernatural re-creation thread. In the Burmese version, the different nations spring out of blood, rather than the hero's piety, but the thread is still strong. The main *difference*, of course, is the appearance of the elves, or what I call the first *externally present creatures*. This means that, despite the "worldwide destruction" of the Flood, some animals (or elves, in this case) survived. This is also a thread that will begin to show up more and more.

Continuing south into Timor, we encounter the Rotti version of the Flood. Here we see the idea of various animals being used as a means of bringing about dry land. This is a peculiar version of the "litmus test" thread because, rather than use the animals to "test" for dry land, they are using the animals in an attempt to *create* dry land, or cause the dry land to appear. We also find the osprey — or "bird thread" — here, but it also contains the "external creature" thread, in that the osprey comes from *outside* of the Flood mountain. These ever-present but ever-changing threads could be a *direct result* of the diaspora.

From Timor, our spread of cultures splits again. One branch heads east, toward New Guinea, while the other heads south into Australia. These branches bring us to the New Guinea and Lake Tyers versions.

The New Guinea version is interesting, because we find the idea of a "magical" or "supernatural" fish — like that in the Sanskrit myth — appearing. What I believe this depicts is a *direct connection* between the Valman myth of New Guinea, and the Hindu myth of India. The fact that treating the fish well saves Manu, and treating the fish poorly destroys the village, is too much of a coincidence. This may very well indicate that a thread of people passed down the "Fish Myth," just as the Flood myth in general may have been passed down from the Genesis version.

In the Lake Tyers region of Victoria, Australia, we see, first and foremost, the appearance of a post-diluvian rescue. This is important, because it shows up later. While it may be an evolution of the "external creature" thread, it may also simply be one of those changes that came about on its own, without any direct link. However, as mentioned before, it does show up again, and in an unlikely place.

As you'll recall, the spread of cultures split shortly before reaching Burma. We have followed the southern branches to their extent. Now, we turn to the northern branches. This migration traveled up the eastern coast of Russia, across the Bering Strait, and into North America. At the border of current-day Alaska, the migration splits in two, one branch moving southeast, the other directly south. Following the southern branch, we arrive in British Columbia where we come to the Kaska version of the Flood.

The Later Versions

The Kaska version combines the Flood with the diaspora. I like that. Could a society plausibly invent such a story? Of course. Actually, that makes sense. One culture would be curious about the origin of the other cultures around it and would make up a story to explain it. That, however, is not the right question to ask. What we should be asking is whether or not this society, plus the other dozen or so we've looked at, plus the hundreds of others that we have not considered, could invent this. If one culture in the world told a story of the world being united under one common language, and then splitting into various other cultures, we could, reasonably, claim it to be an invention. If one culture in the world told a story of a global deluge that preceded this split, we could reasonably claim that to be an invention, as well. However, if several hundred cultures from around the world each tell of a global deluge, followed by a scattering of the nations — some of which *combine* the stories into one tale — can we reasonably claim the legend to be an invention? We'll come back to this.

Moving eastward from British Columbia toward the Hudson Bay, we find the Montagnais version of the Flood. The Hudson Bay version also places the family in a vessel, but here we see the "litmus test" for land transform from birds into other wildlife. We also find that, once dry land appears, the hero places a reindeer on the land and has it circle the island until it is complete. This idea is also important.

Continuing south, we would encounter the Hareskin version. The Hareskin version is very similar to the Australian version in that the hero (a human instead of a pelican) collects the drowning animals two by two (still reminiscent of the Genesis version) as he floats past them. If the groups of migrating people split somewhere around Burma, then we would expect some threads of the story to continue south (into Australia), and other threads to spread north (into the United States). Does the presence of this post-diluvian rescue prove that?

No.

Does it *suggest* it?

Yes.

Lastly, of course, we find the Kariña version, which contains the eight crew members and the animals, but *also* contains the divine re-creation. What does that mean for us? It means that — if we view the development of cultures the way we would play the telephone game — stories change as they are passed on. As new threads are added (the idea of a divine re-creation, for example), they would begin appearing in *unlikely* places. We would also see common threads that cannot be explained if each version were *invented*, separately, by different cultures.

Please bear in mind, as well, that many other versions have not even been addressed. It is not as if the story leaves India and does not appear again until we reach Burma; there are other examples of the myth along the way. I have simply chosen several of these stories out of, literally, hundreds. Because of this, I deeply encourage you to study some of these other versions that we have not considered, and see what parallels you can draw.

Do we then still shake our heads, mutter something about the story being "impossible," and go on with our lives? Perhaps we should, instead, actually take a moment to consider the vast array of mythology that is available to us, and wonder if maybe, *just maybe*, our own history is embedded in there.

Endnotes
1. K. Santon and L. McKay, ed., *Atlas of World History* (Bath, UK: Parragon Publishing, 2005), p. 12–13.

Chapter 13

FINAL THOUGHTS

The man who hears this will dwell in happiness.
— *Mahābhārata,* book III: chapter 185, verse 54

We've taken in a lot of information in these last several pages. Some of it is fairly solid logic, some of it is plausible speculation, and some of it, admittedly, is nothing *but* speculation. But the details should never weigh us down. Rather, we should stay focused on the main issue here: the literature tells us that, at some point in our ancient past, the world was flooded and only a handful survived. But does the literature leave room for us to believe the story?

This is, ultimately, the question telephone mythology is asking us to answer: do we even believe that there *could have been* a great Flood? Yes, it *is* true that the multiple, often eerily similar, versions indicate a flood *probably* occurred. Yes, it *is* clear that the Deluge, *if* it happened, was truly global, and, yes, we can reasonably and logically disregard a few of the versions as inaccurate. Need we believe, for example, that a pelican paddled about the earth in a canoe, rescuing drowning survivors? On the other hand, can we so quickly discard the idea of a family surviving the Flood in a large, *extremely stable* vessel? Still, is the idea not laughable? After all, aren't the most popular images of the Flood — those of Noah's ark — nothing more than silly little bathtub toys with animals sticking out of every window, ready to tip over at the slightest gust of wind?

We've seen that the sheer mass of mythology pertaining to the Deluge is highly indicative that, at some point in our past, the world was flooded and most of mankind was destroyed, save for a few people. The volume of literature portraying this story also tells us that, whether by the aid of some god, the survivors' own holy powers, or the world's largest floating wildlife preserve, the animals of the earth survived as well.

Still, we choose not to believe. Do we choose not to believe what we read because the evidence is stacked against the story? I hope that is no longer the case (that *should* no longer be the case). We have seen how, despite coming from differing cultures, the stories all share common threads. No, we cannot rightly disbelieve because of lack of literary evidence. Perhaps, then, we choose not to believe because we have difficulty believing in anything pertaining to the supernatural.

For some, this is the case. Since many do not believe in any type of deity — whether it is God, Brahma, or Kaputano — they immediately dismiss *all* versions of the story. Why? The answer is simple: the stories *all* require *the involvement of a god*. In the Fish Story, Brahma *warns* Manu of the catastrophe, and Brahma *saves* Manu during the catastrophe. In Genesis,

God *warns* Noah of the Deluge, and God *saves* Noah from the Deluge. In the Kariña version, Kaputano *warns* them . . . and Kaputano *saves* them. The same is true in Australia, North America, China, Africa, and Europe: almost every version has some supernatural involvement. Without this god, the story *is* impossible. How would the heroes of the Flood have had warning, if not for their god? Furthermore, who would have *sent* the Flood as punishment, if not an angry god?

Because of this, many of us reject the myth. We reject it because we choose not to believe in someone greater than us. I think we also reject it because the stories remind us most of all that, if there is a god, we are held accountable for our actions. We often wish to live in a consequence-free environment where our actions have no penalties. The Bible calls these penalties *justice*. The Hindus call them *karma*. But accountability is not popular and therefore we ignore it. Accountability is not popular and therefore we fictionalize it. Accountability is not popular and therefore we *symbolize* it.

This is, frankly, poor and — I am afraid — *lazy* thinking. We have evidence supporting a story, and we have a story supporting the existence of a deity. What happens when we do not believe in a divine being? That means that we now have a choice: dismiss the evidence because of our belief, or *change* our belief because of the evidence. Which is more logically sound?

And *still* we reject the story.

What about those who do believe in a god and still reject the story? For those people, I have no explanation. There are many who claim to follow the Bible but disbelieve the clear, unambiguous teachings of the Flood. Why? I have no idea. Either way, though, it amounts to the same: we disbelieve, simply because we *choose* to disbelieve.

Suppose a good friend of yours — someone who is generally reliable — called you while you were on your way to work yesterday morning. She was hysterical, crying . . . the whole works. The one thing she kept repeating was that she had seen an elephant walking down the main road of your city. Would you believe her? Maybe, but probably not, no matter how reliable she may have been in the past; it is an *elephant*, after all, and elephants don't normally go traipsing through the city. No sooner do you hang up with her, however, than your husband calls. He claims that he saw an elephant heading down one of the side roads of the city, not too far from where your friend says she spotted the pachyderm. Do you believe him? Probably, but maybe not; he may be your husband, but that does *not* automatically make his story plausible! Let's say you arrived at work, and one of your co-workers is *also* crying — just a real mess. She says she was frightened half to death by a near collision with a large gray elephant on the way to work. This elephant was on a different street than the one your husband claims to have seen, and a mile or so from the main street where your friend encountered the elephant. Now, here's the question: do you believe your co-worker? The stories *do* differ slightly, but they also have a pretty common theme, and so you might not believe the story, *exactly*, but you would at least be tempted to investigate further. Now, what if *10* different people told you that an elephant was loose in the city? How about *20*? Would you believe it then?

An oft-referenced work in this book has been Theodore Gaster's *Myth, Legend, and Custom in the Old Testament*. In it, Gaster gives *more than 65* examples of Deluge stories from around the world, not including the three primary versions we have considered here, nor does it include some of the *other* hundreds of versions that are also out there. The stories come from every continent and every major people group. They all agree on one important point: the world was flooded, and only a handful of people survived.

How long do we continue to ignore it? How long do we turn our blind (but "enlightened") intellects away? How long do we scoff at what our ancestors have *all* tried to tell us? How long do we, like Sisyphus, push against our very intellects, trying to put the flood myth where *we* think it deserves to be? How long can we play this game before it finally rolls down on top of us, when we realize — too late — what it was we were vainly hoping to accomplish?

Thinking More Broadly

Contrary to what many may believe upon reading this work, this is not about "proving" a global flood. It reaches deeper, asking us to abandon preconceived ideas and to *think*. We should be willing to look for *connections* — not only those connections that dwell in metaphor, but also the kind that dwell in *history*. When we take a story at face value — that a global Flood occurred, for example, and the survivors then scattered throughout the earth — we open up an entirely new field of interpretive thought. Unfortunately, by "selling out" — immediately disregarding all myth as either fiction or a symbolic representation of the truth — we potentially miss out on our own history.

Is the story of the Flood another *Iliad?* Is it destined to be another Kraken legend? Do we shrug our shoulders and dismiss it simply because someone, somewhere, tells us it isn't true? Or do we take warning from it and seek out the truth of our existence? If Someone were angry enough to wipe out mankind by a global catastrophe, might that same Someone be trying to get our attention in other ways today?

Where do we go from here? That is entirely up to you. Talk to the person who handed you this book. If you picked this book up yourself somewhere, do more research on your own. All I ask is that you not be afraid to believe in something just because it is "religious"; religion and logic are not necessarily opposites, and "faith" and "thought" are not contradictory terms. Don't hide from the *Mahābhārata* just because you're not Hindu, and certainly don't disregard the Bible just because you are an atheist. There may be more truth there than you realize.

Appendix A

PRIMARY TEXTS

The Flood According to the Torah (Gen. 6:9–9:17)

This is the line of Noah. — Noah was a righteous man; he was blameless in his age; Noah walked with God. — Noah begot three sons: Shem, Ham, and Japheth.

The earth became corrupt before God; the earth was filled with lawlessness. When God saw how corrupt the earth was, for all flesh had corrupted its way on earth, God said to Noah, "I have decided to put an end to all flesh, for the earth is filled with all lawlessness because of them: I am about to destroy them with the earth. Make yourself an ark of gopher wood; make it an ark with compartments, and cover it inside and out with pitch. This is how you shall make it: the length of the ark shall be three hundred cubits, its width fifty cubits, and its height thirty cubits. Make an opening for daylight in the ark, and terminate it within a cubit of the top.[1] Put the entrance to the ark on its side; make it with bottom, second, and third decks.

"For My part, I am about to bring the Flood — waters upon the earth — to destroy all flesh under the sky in which there is breath of life; everything on earth shall perish. But I will establish My covenant with you, and you shall enter the ark, with your sons, your wife, and your sons' wives. And of all that lives, of all flesh, you shall take two of each into the ark to keep alive with you; they shall be male and female. From birds of every kind, cattle of every kind, every kind of creeping thing on earth, two of each shall come to you and stay alive. For your part, take of everything that is eaten and store it away, to serve as food for you and for them." Noah did so; just as God commanded him, so he did.

Then the LORD said to Noah, "Go into the ark, with all your household, for you alone have I found righteous before Me in this generation. Of every clean animal you shall take seven pairs, males and their mates, and of every animal that is not clean, two, a male and its mate; of the birds of the sky also, seven pairs, male and female, to keep seed alive upon all the earth. For in seven days' time I will make it rain upon the earth, forty days and forty nights, and I will blot out from the earth all existence that I created." And Noah did just as the LORD commanded him. . . .

In the six hundredth year of Noah's life, in the second month, on the seventeenth day of the month, on that day

All the fountains of the great deep burst apart,

And all the floodgates of the sky broke open.

(The rain fell on the earth forty days and forty nights.) That same day Noah and Noah's sons, Shem, Ham, and Japheth, went into the ark, with Noah's wife and the three wives of his sons — they and all the beasts of every kind. . . . They came to

Noah into the ark, two of each of all flesh in which there was breath of life. . . .

The Flood continued forty days on the earth, and the waters increased and raised the ark so that it rose above the earth. The waters swelled and increased greatly upon the earth, and the ark drifted upon the waters. When the water had swelled much more upon the earth, all the highest mountains everywhere under the sky were covered. Fifteen cubits higher did the waters swell, as the mountains were covered. And all the flesh that stirred on earth perished — birds, cattle, beasts, and all the things that swarmed upon the earth, and all mankind. All in whose nostrils was the merest breath of life, all that was on dry land, died. All existence on earth was blotted out — man, cattle, creeping things, and birds of the sky; they were blotted out from the earth. Only Noah was left, and those with him in the ark.

And when the waters had swelled upon the earth one hundred and fifty days, God remembered Noah and all the beasts and all the cattle that were with him in the ark, and God caused a wind to blow across the earth, and the waters subsided. The fountains of the deep and the floodgates of the sky were stopped up, and the rain from the sky was held back; the waters then receded steadily from the earth. At the end of one hundred and fifty days the water diminished; so that in the seventh month, on the seventeenth day of the month, the ark came to rest on the mountains of Ararat. The waters went on diminishing until the tenth month; in the tenth month, on the first day of the month, the tops of the mountains became visible.

At the end of forty days, Noah opened the window of the ark that he had made and sent out the raven; it went to and fro until the waters had dried up from the earth. Then he sent out the dove to see whether the waters had decreased from the surface of the ground. But the dove could not find a resting place for its foot, and returned to him to the ark, for there was water all over all the earth. So putting out his hand, he took it into the ark with him. He waited another seven days, and again sent out the dove from the ark. The dove came back to him toward the evening, and there in its bill was a plucked-off olive leaf! Then Noah knew that the waters had decreased on the earth. He waited still another seven days and sent the dove forth; and it did not return to him anymore.

In the six hundred and first year, in the first month, on the first of the month, the waters began to dry from the earth; and when Noah removed the covering of the ark, he saw that the surface of the ground was drying. And in the second month, on the twenty-seventh day of the month, the earth was dry.

God spoke to Noah, saying, "Come out of the ark, together with your wife, your sons, and your sons' wives. Bring out with you every living thing of all flesh that is with you: birds, animals, and everything that creeps on the earth; and let them swarm on the earth and be fertile and increase on earth." So Noah came out, together with his sons, his wife, and his sons' wives. Every animal, every creeping thing, and every bird, everything that stirs on earth came out of the ark by families.

Then Noah built an altar to the LORD and, taking of every clean animal and of every clean bird, he offered burnt offerings on the altar. The LORD smelled the pleasing odor, and the LORD said to Himself: "Never again will I doom the earth because of man, since the devisings of man's mind are evil from his youth; nor will I ever again destroy every living being, as I have done.

> So long as the earth endures,
>> Seedtime and harvest,
>> Cold and heat,
>> Summer and winter,
>> Day and night
>> Shall not cease."

God blessed Noah and his sons, and said to them, "Be fertile and increase, and fill the earth. The fear and the dread of you shall be upon all the beasts of the earth and upon all the birds of the sky — everything with which the earth is astir — and upon all the fish of the sea; they are given into your hand. Every creature that lives shall be yours to eat; as with the green grasses, I give you all these. . . ."

God further said, "This is the sign that I set for the covenant between Me and you, and every living creature with you, for all the ages to come. I have set My bow in the clouds, and it shall serve as a sign of the covenant between Me and the earth. When I bring clouds over the earth, and the bow appears in the clouds, I will remember My covenant between Me and you and every living creature among all flesh, so that the waters shall never again become a flood to destroy all flesh. . . . That," God said to Noah, "shall be the sign of the covenant that I have established between Me and all flesh that is on earth."[2]

The Flood According to The *Mahābhārata*

Vaśampāyana said:

"Then the mighty Pāṇḍava said to Mārkaṇḍeya, 'Tell me, I implore, the life of Manu-Vaivasvata.'

"Mārkaṇḍeya said, 'There was a glorious king of the Ṛsis, son of Vivasvata, who was a prominent man with a brilliance equal to that of Prajāpati. Exceeding the brilliance of his own father and grandfather with vigor, splendor, fortune, and, above all, piety, Manu the king, standing in the garden of penance on one foot with his extensive arms raised, performed completely and passionately the greatest of all pious rituals, the *tapas*. So with his head hung down and his eyes unblinking, he performed this frightful penance for a thousand years, bearing wet clothes and matted hair.

" 'Once, having come to the bank of the river, a fish said the following speech: "O Lord, I am just a little fish, and I am very much afraid of the other fish. You are respectable, and will protect me. The mighty fish eat, in particular, the feeble fish. This is common practice." . . . Manu-Vaivasvata, having heard the words of the fish, was filled with compassion, and drew out the fish with his own hands onto the shore of the river. Manu placed the moon-colored fish into a small jar. The fish grew, and during this time, he was treated with the same honor as Manu's own son.

" 'With time, the great fish grew bigger in the small jar of water, and, assuredly, spoke to Manu, "Virtuous Lord, you have looked over me with care. Grant me that I may live in comfort and peace." Then the illustrious Manu, conqueror of cities, drew the fish from the jar, and placed the fish into a reservoir.[3] Again, many years passed.

" 'The reservoir was two *yojas*[4] in length, and one *yoja* in width, and was not enough room for the fish to move, O Lord.[5] Manu, having seen the fish, was again spoken to: "My Lord, throw me into the Chief Wife of the Ocean. There, in the Ganges, I will reside as your son."

" 'Thus, having heard the fish, Manu, the self-controlled lord, threw the fish into the Ganges. There, over time, the fish grew and, having seen Manu again, said, "Truly, Lord, having grown here in the Ganges, I am unable to move. Place me in the sea, my Lord."

" 'Having drawn the fish from the waters of the Ganges, son of Pṛthā, Manu personally placed him in the ocean. The fish was very large, but Manu the Intelligent loved the feel and smell of the fish, and easily did as the fish wished. When the fish had been thrown into the sea by Manu, he smiled and said, "Lord, having done this, and having taken care of me with all distinction, listen to me, so that you may do what is necessary.

" ' "Soon, Fortune-favored Lord, the dissolution of all moving and unmoving things of earth is near. This Deluge of the worlds is approaching. I know this, so that you may have the advantage today. Of the mobile, the immobile, and of this that moves and that which is stationary, all ends in violent water. A boat[6] is to be built by you, furnished with a sturdy cord. There, with the seven Ṛsis, sit, Great Manu, and take with you all the seeds, as spoken of by the Brahmins long ago, preserving them in portions.

" ' "Remain in the boat and wait for me, and be protected from the desolation by my affection. I will come as a horned creature. Do what is required of you. I must go. You must anticipate my return, and heed my words."

" 'He responded to the fish, "This will be done." The two parted. Then, Great King, Manu did as the fish said. Having taken all the seeds, he crossed the ocean in the boat. And Manu thought of the fish, O King, and the fish, knowing his thought, came there, Great Bharata, as a horned creature, going before the boat.

" 'Having seen that fish with the shape of a horned creature, Manu, the king and lord of men, tossed the cord over the forehead of the fish. Manu, distinguished among men, tossed the cord onto the horn of the fish. With the fish going ahead, the great boat was drug through the salty water by the impetus of the cord. In this way, the Lord of Men crossed the ocean, with his boat dancing angrily with the thundering waves and violent winds. The boat, O Conqueror of Distant Cities,[7] rolled about, staggering like a drunk prostitute. In all directions, neither the earth nor the sky were seen. All was sea, Best Among Men, and only Manu, the Fish, and the seven Ṛsis could be seen then in that disordered earth, Most Excellent of Bharatas.

" 'O King, the fish pulled the boat carefully through the flood waters for many years, finally dragging it to the highest peak of the Himalayas. Then the fish said to the Ṛsis, with slight irony,[8] "Bind the boat quickly to the peak of the Himalayas." Having heard the words of the fish, the boat was quickly tied there by the Ṛsis, on the peak of the Himalayas. That highest peak is called, even to this day, *Naubandhanam*.⁹ This you know, Son of Kunti, Best Among Bharatas. Then the god said to the assembly of the Ṛsis, 'I am the Creator Brahma, Most High, Unattainable, and you have, by me, been set free from danger, having attained for myself the form of a fish. And now, all men, gods, and demons, all things earthly, those that move, and those which are stationary, will be created by Manu. And by the intensity of his piety, he will obtain power, and, in the abandonment of confusion, will *not* go to disillusionment.' Thus, having spoken these words, the fish disappeared, and Manu-Vaivasvata was filled with the desire to create men. In the process of creating, he became bewildered. Then, with the great meditation of *tapas*, he was joined with God. Manu began to create all men, Best of Bharatas.

" 'This story is called the Fish Myth. The ancient tale, having been spoken by me, recounts the expurgation of evil. The man who hears this will dwell in happiness, and will go to whichever heavenly world he desires.' "¹⁰

The Flood According to the Kariña Peoples

In days long-past, the sky-god, Kaputano, came down to the kingdom of the Kariña. "Children," he called, "hear me well! Soon, a great rain will fall upon the earth, and will cover all with water."

Out of everyone there, however, only four couples were afraid. When they heard his words, they listened, though the rest scoffed.

"I am your father and your god," he insisted. "I desire that none of you should perish. I will help you build a canoe that will hold everyone, so that no one drowns."

"You are not Kaputano," they said, "and there is no flood." But the four couples, scared half out of their wits, listened to what he said. The rest continued to make fun of him.

"So be it," said Kaputano.

Then Kaputano, with the other eight people, began to build a very large canoe. It was a great canoe, and when they were done, they went about gathering two of each animal to put on board. They also brought seeds from every plant on earth.

The moment everyone was on board, the sky grew black. The wind picked up, the earth shook, and it began to rain. It rained and rained. The rain kept on for many, many days. It rained so hard, the rivers overflowed. Water was everywhere, and all the animals outside were swept away. There was so much water, not even the tops of the tallest trees were visible. Those Kariña who were outside — those who would not believe Kaputano — could not be rescued, and they were drowned. The waves came and came, and they were so high that the entire world was covered.

Many days later, when the waters began to recede and the land began to dry, the four couples exited the canoe. They looked at their world. It was void and empty, with nothing to be seen. Kaputano asked them, "Do you like it like this, or would you want something different? How do you want it to look?"

The Kariña told him that no one could survive in a place like this. "Where are the trees?" they asked. "How are we to weave baskets, and make roofs for our houses, if there aren't any palm leaves? How are we supposed to grow food, without mountain slopes? Where is there shelter?"

So Kaputano, out of love for his children, created a new earth for the Kariña. He filled it with rivers and trees, lakes and marshes, mountains and hills. And the Kariña lived there forever, happy and content.[11]

Endnotes

1. The meaning of this Hebrew phrase is uncertain.

2. Gen. 6:9–9:17, *Tanakh* (Jewish Publication Society, Philadelphia, PA).
3. Or possibly "man-made-pond."
4. A *yoja* is equal to about 9.5 English miles.
5. Remember, the story is being narrated to Pāṇḍava.
6. Also translated "raft."
7. Another name for Pāṇḍava.
8. The meaning of this phrase is unclear.
9. The name means "anchored ship."
10. *Mahābhārata* III:185/1–54.
11. Based on *The Great Canoe: A Kariña Legend*, by Maria Elena Maggi.

Appendix B

SECONDARY SOURCES

The Epic of Gilgamesh, *Babylon*

At this point in the epic, Gilgamesh is seeking the secret to immortality. He hears that one man — Utnapishtim — has achieved immortality by surviving a Global Flood. Intrigued, Gilgamesh seeks out Utnapishtim, who tells him the story.

Utnapishtim said to Gilgamesh, "You are aware of Shurrupak. It is a city on the banks of the Euphrates. The city is old ... ancient ... and, once upon a time, the very gods lived in it. They reveled in its majesty. But, like most things, it soon lost its luster, and they decided to send a flood, such that would destroy all of mankind. Ea, the god of wisdom and subtlety,

All versions are retold based on versions in Theodore Gaster, *Myth, Legend, and Custom in the Old Testament* (New York: Harper & Row, 1969).

was part of their counsel and informed me of their decision. I heard him whistling through my thatched hut." Utnapishtim remembered this, and chuckled. "You see, he told me to look after myself and my belongings. 'Construct a vessel thirty cubits long and thirty cubits wide. Gather a representative of every living thing. Stock it with food and waters, and then launch it upon the ocean.'

" 'What am I to tell my neighbors?' I asked.

" 'Say that Enlil, the god of gods, is angry with you, and has banished you from the city. Tell them that you have decided to leave his realm, heading to sea (which belongs to Ea, anyway). Tell them I will take care of you.'

"I did as told, and designed the vessel, built it, and gathered food, water, and other necessities. When my provisions were collected, I coated the outside with pitch, and the inside with tar. Then I brought my family on board, along with all of our possessions, the provisions for the trip, and two of every animal. That very night, the cloud warriors marched in, pouring down upon the earth a vicious rain, and stirring up a terrifying storm. Having chosen a captain, I placed him at the helm and cut loose the mooring lines, allowing the craft to float free. At dawn, while the sky was still gray, a churning, ink-black cloud moved in from the west as the fury of the gods was unleashed. Adad, with his troops, thundered; Nergal came and tore off my anchor; Ninurta brought death and destruction upon those outside; the Anunaki, those fierce warriors, brandished their torches. The whole sky was black, and you could not see your hand in front of you. Even those gods who remained in their heavenly palaces were afraid; never before had a storm such as this been seen on earth."

Gilgamesh, entranced, leaned forward as Utnapishtim continued. "For nearly a week, the flood swept us on. On the seventh day, however, the raging and battling wind exhausted itself, died down, and, as suddenly as it had begun, the storm ceased. I looked out the window of the ship, to see what I could observe. There was no sound. Everything — including all life — had turned to mud and muck. Nothing could be seen but cloudy, murky water. With the daylight on my face and my heavy, sorrowful heart still beating in my breast, I wept. I wept for those lost. I wept for those of us who remained. Mostly, I wept because the earth was gone. All was water.

"On the twelfth day, I finally saw several small patches of land emerging from the waters. The ship eventually grounded on the slopes of Mount Nişir, where we remained another six days.

"On the seventh day, I let a dove out of the window, to see if it would land. But it found nowhere to rest, and so returned to me. Next, I sent a swallow, but it too returned. Lastly, I sent out a raven. The raven, finding land, never returned.

"At this point, I began to unload my cargo. The first thing I did, upon stepping on dry land was to give an offering to the gods. They smelled the pleasing aroma, and began to swarm around it like flies on honey. Eventually, Ishtar stepped forward and held up her necklace, a multi-colored present from the sky-god.

" 'Behold these jewels!' she called out. 'Just as I will never forget these, so will I never forget what we have seen these last days! I say we all enjoy this feast . . . all of us except Enlil, for it was his idea!'

"Now," continued the old man, "when Enlil saw that I had survived his flood, he was *livid*, and demanded the name of the traitor. Ninurta, I believe it was, commented that since Ea had the gift of foresight, it could only have been him. Besides, Ninurta had argued, Ea was both shrewd and cunning. Ea interrupted at this point, reprehending Enlil for his monstrous brutality and callousness.

" 'Only the guilty should have been destroyed,' he declared, 'and not all of humanity.'

" 'And how,' Enlil asked, 'would this have been accomplished?'

" 'By sending vicious animals, or a plague,' Ea suggested. 'You needn't have killed *everyone*. Besides,' he narrowed his eyes as he spoke these next words, 'I merely gave a hint, like a dream. It's not my fault Utnapishtim is so intelligent, and figured out a plan to survive.'

"Enlil nodded in agreement, for Ea was quite shrewd and persuasive. Then, having assented to Ea's point, he led both my wife and I back on board. Enlil blessed us both, and, as a reward, granted us eternal life. However, it would not do for the immortal to live among the mortal. So he gave us this island, away from all other humanity, where we could spend our days in peace and tranquility."

Something I find interesting is that, similar to the Genesis version, this vessel is also a giant floating box. The difference, of course, is that the Gilgamesh version is a perfect cube, about 40 feet on each side (assuming the height was equal to the sides, which is likely). That gives Utnapishtim's vessel about 64,000 cubic feet of space. Compared to Noah's 500-railway-car volume, Utnapishtim's 200-car volume seems extremely small.

The Flood According to the Kaska Indians of British Columbia

There was once a flood, which covered the whole earth. The sky grew very dark, and the winds kicked up fiercely. Some people quickly took canoes, and others quickly made rafts, and when the wind came, it separated the people, blowing them every which way. When the waters finally receded, the people all found that they had landed far from each other, so that not one family could see another. When the earth became dry enough to build upon, they settled where they had landed. Most people probably thought they were the only ones who had survived. Many years later, when they finally did begin to meet other people, everyone discovered that no one spoke the same language! This is the reason that there are so many tribes and languages. Before the flood, you see, there was but one tribe, and everyone lived together and spoke the same language.

I like this version because of the blending of the Flood story and the dispersion story. In most mythology, the stories are completely separated. In others — as is the case with the Genesis version — the stories are separated but are chained together through other events. It is an interesting perspective to find the two of them combined into one story.

The Story of the Flood According to the Chingpaws, Upper Burma

Once upon a time, a man named Nan-chaung and his sister Chang-hko built a large boat to save themselves from the Deluge. They had with them nine roosters, and nine bone needles. After the storm had raged for many days, they threw over one rooster and one needle, to see if the waters had subsided. The rooster did not crow, however, and, though they listened, the needle was not heard to hit the bottom. Each day, they did the same thing. Finally, on the ninth day, the rooster crowed, and they heard the needle strike the bottom of the water. Shortly thereafter, they were able to leave their boat.

The two of them wandered about until they came upon a cave. Inside the cave lived a male and female elf. The elves asked them to stay, and the couple joined the elves in their work, hauling wood, clearing fields, and so forth. Some time later, the sister gave birth to a child. One day, while the parents were out doing their chores, the old she-elf, who was a witch, was watching the baby. The child began to scream and cry, and the wretched woman threatened to turn it into mince meat pie. But the child did not stop screaming, and the old elf snatched the child, took it to the crossroads, and hacked it to pieces, dripping blood all over the road.

She carried pieces of the child back to the cave, and made them into an enticing curry dish. To hide what she had done, she placed a block of wood in the cradle, and covered it with a blanket. When the parents came in from working, the she-elf told the mother to be quiet, because the baby was sleeping. The mother did as suggested, and the four of them ate their meal of rice and curry. After dinner, however, the mother could stand it no longer, and went to the cradle to hold her baby. But inside, she found the block of wood!

"Where is my baby!" she demanded of the witch.

"You have eaten him!" the witch cackled.

The woman, horrified, fled from the house. As she came to the crossroads, not knowing what had happened there just a few hours earlier, she dropped to her knees and wailed to the Great Spirit, "Please give me my baby back!" The Great Spirit, saddened by all that had taken place, came to her. "I cannot put your baby back together," he explained, "but instead I will make you mother of all men. " And as he said this, people sprang up from the road, a different group of people wherever the blood had touched the ground. And so, because each group came from her baby, she was, indeed, the mother of all men.

Though this version is gruesome, it offers something none of the other versions offer: post-diluvian survivors. I, personally, am not comfortable with the accuracy of this version, simply because the point of the global Flood was to wipe out all other life. However, the whimsical idea of a couple of elves surviving the Flood is rather comical, sort of Tolkien meets the Brothers Grimm.

The Flood According to the Bahnars, China

Once, a crab and a kite had an argument. The kite pecked the crab so hard that he pierced the crab's shell. To avenge this great insult, the crab caused the waters of the sea to swell. They swelled so much that everything on earth was destroyed, except for two people: a brother and a sister. The brother and sister managed to survive by locking themselves in a huge chest. Because they were afraid that everything would perish forever, they brought on board two of every animal. After seven days and seven nights of listening to the raging waters, the brother and sister heard a cock crowing outside, and knew that it was safe to leave the chest (they knew that the ancestors had sent the cock, to tell them when it was safe to come out). So they opened the lid and let all the birds fly out. Then they let all the other animals out. Finally, they left the chest, as well. They were dismayed, however, because they had eaten all the rice that was on board, and would have starved to death if an ant had not brought them two grains of rice. They planted the rice, and in the morning, it had grown until it filled the entire field.

I must admit that I can't quite figure out the inclusion of the battle between the crab and the kite. Did this detail emerge over time, or was it one of those spontaneous changes that happens when one is retelling a story? Perhaps the Bahnars used to start with the swelling of the sea, but some inquisitive child asked why the seas swelled, forcing the storyteller to improvise a reason. And maybe that reason simply stuck. Though I laugh at the idea of an angry crab causing the Flood . . . it's very Aesop.

The Story of Deucalion, Greece

Deucalion was the son of Prometheus, and he ruled in Phthia. His wife, Pyrrah, was the daughter of Epimetheus and Pandora (it was Pandora who was the first woman to be created by the gods). One day, Prometheus came to Deucalion and told him, "Zeus is going to destroy all the men of this Bronze Age. Build yourself a chest of wood, so that you and your wife may survive."

Deucalion did just that, and after he had provisioned it, took his wife aboard with him. At this time, Zeus opened the floodgates of the sky, and poured a terrible rain down upon the earth. All the men of Greece were killed, save a few, which made Zeus even angrier. So he parted the great mountains of Thessaly, flooding the entire world beyond both the Isthmus and the Peloponnesian realm. Deucalion, however, in his chest of wood, lived comfortably on the sea for nine days and nine nights. Eventually, the chest came to rest on Parnassus, and, when the rains stopped, Deucalion sacrificed to Zeus. Zeus, pleased by the sacrifice, granted Deucalion one choice — to name anything that he may desire. Deucalion chose men, because he did not want to remain alone on earth. So, at the command of Zeus, he picked up stones and threw them over his head. The stones he threw became men, and the stones Pyrrah threw became women. This is why people are called *laoi*, from *laas*, "a stone."

I specifically left in the detail that Zeus wanted to destroy all the men of the "Bronze Age." This detail makes the events of this version — along with the Genesis version — easy to date, within a reasonable window. In Hebrew chronology, the Flood would have occurred roughly 3000 B.C. The Greek version, which we're told ended the Bronze Age, would have happened around 4000 B.C.[2]

The Montagnais People, Hudson Bay

A race of giants was destroying the earth, and God, angry with them for it, commanded a man to build a very large canoe. The man did as he was told, and as soon as he entered it, the water rose on all sides, until no land could be seen in any direction. Bored with the scenery, the man told an otter to dive down into the waters and see what he could find. The otter returned with a piece of earth. The man took the earth in his hand and breathed on it, and it began to grow. So he laid it on the water, kept it from sinking, and watched as it continued to grow. As it grew and grew, the man saw that it was becoming an island. So he placed a reindeer on it, and the reindeer ran around in a circle, making a quick circuit about the island. The man decided that the earth was not yet large enough, so he continued to blow on it. In time, all of the lakes, mountains, and rivers were formed, and the man knew it was time to leave the canoe.

What is interesting here is that in Genesis, in an earlier chapter, we find that a race of giants has been born on the earth, and it is hinted that these giants are part of the corrupting force that warrants the Deluge. Since first preparing this manuscript, I have come across several South American versions of the Flood, many of which also include this pre-diluvian race of giants.

The Flood According to the Valmans, Berlin Harbour, New Guinea

Once upon a time, the wife of a noble man saw a fish. She called to her husband, but by the time he got there, the fish had gone. So she had him hide behind a banana tree, in case the fish came back. At last, peering through the leaves of the tree, the man caught sight of the fish. He was immediately afraid and commanded everyone in the village to stay away from the fish.

A certain wicked man, however, would not listen, and so shot at the fish with an arrow. The good man, when he saw this, drove a pair of every animal into the tree and climbed into it with his family. Meanwhile, the wicked man had prepared the fish and was eating it. No sooner had he finished eating than water sprang out of the ground, reaching to the top of the tree. It flooded the entire land, killing everyone. Then the waters subsided, and the man, his family, and the animals he had saved came out of the tree.

Though this version appears to be a local flood legend, the parallels to other versions were too strong to resist inclusion. I particularly like the appearance of the fish in this version. I also like the animals being forced into the tree, mostly because it's plain silly.

The Flood According to the Hareskin Indians, North America

A Wise Man, long ago, decided to build a large raft. His wife watched him build it for several days. Finally, she asked him, "Why do you build a great raft?"

"Because," he answered, "I foresee a terrible catastrophe. The earth will flood, and we shall all take refuge on my raft." But when he told his plan to his neighbors, they all laughed at him. The Wise Man, nonetheless, continued to build his raft. He placed large logs side by side. Then he twisted roots together to make a sturdy rope, and used the rope to lash the trees together.

Without warning, a flood such as has never been seen before came upon the people of earth. Water came at them from every direction, and though men climbed trees, the water continued to rise, eventually washing them all away until everyone had drowned. The Wise Man, however, floated safely with his wife, who was also his sister, in their strong and sturdy raft. As he floated, it occurred to him that all of the animals would drown, too. So as he floated, he gathered pairs of all of the tame animals, the birds, and even the beasts of prey.

The earth was eventually gone. It disappeared under the water, and for many weeks, no one even considered going to look for it. The first to dive in was the muskrat, but swim as he might, he never reached the bottom. By the time he returned to the surface, he was nearly drowned to death! When he had caught his breath, he told the Wise Man that the earth was not to be found. After a few days, he tried again. This time, when he returned, he reported that he could smell the earth but could not touch it.

On the third attempt, the beaver tried. He kicked fast and hard and was gone for a very long time. At last, to every-one's relief, he appeared. Though he was much out of breath and nearly unconscious, he was holding in his paw a bit of mud. The Wise Man thanked the beaver, took the mud, and placed it in the water. He leaned over the edge of the raft and breathed on the mud, whispering, "I wish for there to be land once more!" At that moment, the mud began to grow. The Wise Man placed a small bird on the patch of mud, and the mud did not sink. In fact, it continued to grow. So he breathed on it again and put a fox on it. Still the mud grew, and the fox ran around it in a single day.

Around and around the fox went, and the island contin-ued to grow bigger and bigger. The fox ran around the island six times, but by the seventh time around, the land was com-plete, as if the flood had never even happened. Then the Wise Man unloaded all of the animals, and they walked, for the first time in a long time, on dry ground. Last of all came the man, his wife, and their son, and soon afterwards, the earth was re-peopled.

I like the very practical aspect of building the raft. The fact that we are told how he made the rope is, at least to me, fascinating. Many of the flood myths tend to leave out some of the more practical details, and it's interesting to see these in what would otherwise be a very impractical version.

The Flood According to the Rotti, Timor

Once, the sea-god became angry with mankind and decided to flood the whole earth. In fact, the entire earth was destroyed, except for the peak of one mountain. A man and his sister, along with several animals, escaped to the high mountain, and there survived. However, there was nowhere to go. So they asked the sea-god to bring the waters back down. The sea-god answered them: "I will bring the waters back down, but only if you can throw me a creature whose hairs I cannot number."

So the man and his wife threw a pig into the waves, but the sea-god could number the hairs of the pig. So they then threw in a goat, but the sea-god could count those, too. They then threw in a dog, and then a hen, but the sea-god counted both of them. Finally, they threw in a cat, and this was more than the sea-god could take. So he agreed that the waters would be returned to their place. After that, an osprey flew over the mountain, sprinkling dirt on the water. The dirt became dry land, and the man and his sister were able to descend the mountain.

I almost did not include this version at all, simply because the man and his sister/wife escape to a high mountain, indicating that the flood could not have been global. However, since the text does say, in no uncertain terms, that the entire earth was flooded, we can chalk this inconsistency up to the watering down of the original flood myth.

The Flood According to the Aborigines of Lake Tyers, Victoria

Once upon a time, a huge frog swallowed all the water of the world, and everyone was thirsty. The plants were parched, and the fish were most put out by the inconvenience; they flopped about on the dry land, gasping for air. Because of this, all the animals took a poll and decided that the best way to make the frog give back the water was to make him laugh. So they all stood in front of him, playing pranks and cutting up. They were so hilarious that anyone else would have died laughing, but the frog did not even smile. Stoic as ever, he sat curled up in a dreadfully drab silence, with his big eyes and swollen, water-filled cheeks. Finally, as a last resort, the eel wriggled about, dancing and swaying as it stood up on its tail. Not even the glum frog could watch this without laughing. He laughed and he laughed until tears ran down his cheeks. The water poured from his mouth and soon became a flood. The waters rose, killing many people. In fact, all of mankind would have drowned, if the pelican had not paddled about in a canoe, rescuing survivors as he went.

This version is just plain fun. The thought of an eel dancing on its tail, wriggling about in front of a giant frog, just makes me laugh. I can see why the ornery amphibian finally released the water. Of course, this idea of the pelican rescuing people — instead of the other way around — is an interesting reversal, in that it does tend to steal some credibility from this version. Obviously, a pelican did not paddle about rescuing mankind. This is, perhaps, one of the strongest arguments that the Australian version is not the accurate version. The most likely scenario is that the actual Flood involved people rescuing animals, and those details reversed as the story began to spread and change into folklore.

Endnotes

1. K. Santon and L. McKay, ed., *Atlas of World History* (Bath, UK: Parragon Publishing, 2005), p. 17.

Appendix C

THE MYTH OF
APOLLO'S CHARIOT

At this point in the narrative, Phaëthon, product of the union between the goddess Clymene and the sun-god Phoebus Apollo, has approached his father's house to determine if he truly is the son of Apollo. The visit is prompted by a harsh teasing from several of Phaëthon's playmates, and the encouragement of his mother to find out the truth for himself. This version of the myth is my own retelling, taken from several different English translations.

The palace of the Sun is wide, open, and lofty, with sweeping columns, bright luminous gold, and burnished bronze that glows like fire. Ivory adorns the staircase, and the doorways are silver that has been shined and polished to look like glass. Everywhere one may turn one's head, the artwork is more splendid than any precious metal and rarer than any gemstone. On the doors, Vulcan — most noble of all artisans — has carved an elaborate and detailed picture. The island of the earth sits within the ocean that surrounds it. Above, on its column of clouds, sits heaven. The details of the carving are exquisite, with no intricacy overlooked: in the sea is Triton, lord of the waves and tides, singing his sea chanteys. Proteus is there, as is the wrestler, Aegaeon, and Doris with her 50 Nereid daughters. Her lovely girls, distinct in face and form, do a variety of activities: some sit on rocks, basking in the sun and combing their long green hair, while others ride through the waves on the backs of dolphins and porpoises. Though they are still clearly sisters, no two are alike in appearance and beauty.

On the land, Vulcan had carved great cities, sweeping fields, plants, animals, men, monsters, and even the demigods who rule over the rivers. Above the earth, in the sky, were carved all the planets, stars, and the 12 signs of the zodiac. The zodiac signs were depicted 6 on each of the doors.

The road to the palace was steep, but Phaëthon climbed boldly, approaching his father's house with both fear and confidence. As he entered the hall, he had to shield his eyes, for even at this distance, his father's face was too bright to behold. His father, Phoebus — if what his mother told him was true — sat enthroned in a chair of emerald, dressed in a fine robe of purple. He was surrounded by his attendants: Day, Month, Year, and Century. The Hours scurried to and fro on their endless, menial tasks, while the more noble Seasons chatted and conversed among themselves. Phaëthon spotted Spring in her blossom diadem, Summer dressed in sprigs of grain, Fall wearing the joyful splotches of trodden grapes, and chilly Winter with his flowing white hair and cascading beard. At the very center of this sat the Sun, his dazzling eyes piercing his offspring's soul, beholding the terrified youth who stood awestruck at the majesty now surrounding him.

"My son," Apollo said warmly, "you are welcome in this house. But tell me, what brings you here? Whatever could be on your mind? Speak, lad, and tell your father."

The boy took a moment, but at last found his voice. "Light of the world," he began, approaching the throne, "if I may be permitted to address you in such a fashion, I have come here to hear you declare me your son, and provide me with a token of that declaration. My mind is troubled, and I seek reassurance."

His father removed his radiant crown, invited his son to come nearer to him, and embraced him. At long last, releasing Phaëthon, the god said, "You are, indeed, my son. Clymene has not lied to you, and I shall prove it. As proof, I shall grant you one favor — any favor at all. Whatever you desire or ask for, I shall provide. I swear by the river Styx (or whatever it is the gods swear on, for I myself have never seen that imposing waterway)," here he winked at this remark, "that whatever you ask shall be given to you."

Phaëthon the son requested his father's chariot for the day, and the opportunity to lead that magnificent pair of winged horses. Phoebus grieved that he had ever sworn an oath and shook his resplendent head. "I am sorry I ever made this promise!" he said. "Your request tells me that it was a foolish and vain thing to do. While I cannot retract my promise, I can ask you — beg you — to choose another token. Please, Son! I ask you to choose another favor . . . *any* favor at all!" But Phaëthon shook his head. "Son, please! What you ask for is madness! You are not strong enough to handle the reins, nor are you skilled enough to steer the chariot. You are a mere mortal, and even the gods themselves know that only I can drive this vehicle! I do this for your own good, because I love you! Not even Jove, the god of gods, would dare to take those reins into his hands! Do you understand?"

But Phaëthon shook his head again.

Apollo sighed deeply. "Let me tell you the way of it. The road is at first very steep, much steeper than the gentle incline that brought you here. The horses, as strong as they may be, can barely make the climb — even at the very start of day, when they are at their most rested. As they mount to the sky, they strain and pull on the reins, their very muscles bulging with the effort.

"Once it levels off, however, a new challenge arises. The track is so high that merely looking down on the mountains and glittering seas is enough to make the strong of heart faint. I do this every day, but my heart *still* melts, and my knees are like water. On this track are many perils. Throughout the entire journey, the heavens revolve, spinning and whirling in constant motion, and I fight to press on against it. How could you endure this dizzying and nauseating spin? If I can barely keep pace, would you not be swept away?

"In addition, the track is a rough jungle of peril. There are no temples or attractive groves of trees, and no beautiful maidens offering pleasant gifts. There are, instead, fierce beasts waiting to devour you. There is the violent bull, the crab with his razor-sharp claws, the famished lion, and Scorpio, with his deadly poisoned tail. But the last part is the most difficult — compared to it, the rest of the journey is a leisurely stroll through the gardens of Jove.

"The final, sudden and steep descent is barely navigable. You would be taking your own life into your hands with those heavy reins. Each day, Tethys greets me, opening the gates to her waters and inviting me in, and each day, she worries that I may overturn and fall headlong into the sea — as I nearly do every evening.

"And the horses, Phaëthon! They are far from tame, my son! Smoke and brimstone pours from their nostrils, and flames spurt from their mouths. Their necks, muscular and bulging, fight against the harness. Why would you endure this? I cannot change my mind, nor withdraw my promise, but you ask for a fatal gift."

The young man would not sway. Though he heard every word his father spoke, he would not listen. He wanted the chariot. And so, slowly, Phoebus led his son to Vulcan's masterpiece — Apollo's great chariot of fire. Its axles were pure gold, shined and brilliant to behold. The golden handiwork, which was laid upon both the tongue of the cart, as well as the rims of the great wheels, had no equal. Its spokes were purest silver, and the horses' yoke was inlaid with crystals and gems, which reflected the light of the Sun. Phaëthon was speechless as he ascended into the vehicle. He climbed slowly, trembling, as in the east, Aurora opened her purple gates and the stars began to fade in the heavens.

Apollo watched with dread as the last horns of the moon descended from view, and he ordered the Hours to harness the steeds. As the morning star — last to leave its watch — dwindled, the goddess led the fiery horses from their stalls. Well-rested, they snorted and stamped the ground, sending sparks and flames into the air. Their bridles were buckled, and the yoke was laid upon their backs. Phoebus Apollo rubbed a balm on his son to protect him from the heat and fire. Then, in spite of his godly stature, sighed heavily as he placed the brilliant Diadem of the Sun on the boy's head.

"Phaëthon," he said, "if you will not change your mind, then take my advice. *Never* use the whip! The whip would only drive them mad. Instead, keep the pace as slow and steady as you can, and keep tight control on these feisty animals. Even with them restrained, the ride will be exciting enough. The course is an arc, running through the realms of the heavens. The wheels have worn ruts in the path over the years. Follow those. Don't go too high, which would set the heavens ablaze. Neither swing too low, for you would burn the earth. Keep to the middle!

Swerve neither to the right nor to the left. On the right is the Serpent, waiting to devour. On the left is heaven's altar. Do not crash into it! I hope Fortune will guide you during this journey. Keep your wits! Do not panic, or things will go poorly. Now, night is at its close, and day is upon us!" He tried one last time to dissuade his son, but Phaëthon would not budge.

The boy stood proudly in the chariot, waved good-bye to his mourning father, thanked him for the gift, and was off. The horses broke into a gallop, their hooves rumbling on the ground, their flames glazing the clouds in their path. The chariot rose ever higher, passing East Wind and ascending into the air. The horses could tell a difference in the weight of the car and took advantage of the lighter load. Just as a ship on the ocean will keel without its usual ballast, the chariot bounded along as an unstable toy in the sky. To the horses, it was as if there was no pilot at all steering the vehicle. The horses, feeling free to frolic and romp at will, broke into the unknown territories of the sky. Apollo had always kept them on the narrow course set for them, but today, there was no restraint.

The young man, panicking, dropped the reins. His resolve had fled — as he would have liked to do — but he could not escape. He knew he was about to die. Looking back, he could see the space in which he had already traveled, but looking ahead, he could see the much longer distance still left. On either side of him were the vicious creatures of the celestial realm. The scorpion prepared to strike, as all scorpions would do. This one, unlike its smaller cousins on earth, blotted out the entire sky. Phaëthon quaked in terror at the sight of the deadly creature and the poison that glistened on the tip of its tail. He gave up all hope of controlling the vehicle, and the reins — briefly regained — fell from his hands.

With this complete freedom, the horses reared up, and, with no boundaries, ran headlong into newer regions of the sky. They had always desired to explore the lands beyond their road, but Apollo had always kept them in check. Now, free, they bolted from the track. The Moon watched, aghast, as her brother's chariot burned up the warriors of rain — the clouds — and the earth caught fire. She watched in horror as mountaintops ignited, and, with mounting dismay, the rocks began to explode. Trees ignited, fields of grain were reduced to ash and dust, and entire cities were engulfed. We cannot imagine what it would look like for an entire nation to ignite, flash, and be gone. It was as if the world had become the hearth of a great fireplace. Woodlands burned, mountains were the great logs, and the springs of earth dried up. Athos, Taurus, Tmolus, Oeta, Ida, Helicon, Haemus, and Aetna: all were gone, burnt up and charred. The mountain snows of Rhodope simmered away, even as the sacred Cithaeron melted into fire. The Scythian ranges — far removed from the center of the calamity — blazed and smoldered. The Caucasus were covered with a thick black cloud. The Alps, jagged and white, were destroyed, and even mighty Olympus burned.

Phaëthon looked at this carnage, his lungs burning with the smoke and heat, in dismay. The car had become a furnace, its bottom radiating heat, charring the soles of his feet, as sparks whirled about him. Heaven had turned into hell. The boy's eyes fried in his head, and his eyelids were seared together, just as a wound is cauterized. It is said that the Ethiopians were burnt up by the intense heat. The Libyan desert, it is said, used to be a tropical paradise before this, and now her rivers and lakes were all boiled away. The nymphs of Libya's pools and springs tore out their hair in mourning. The great Corinthian spring dried up, and all of earth's mighty rivers withdrew in their beds. Poseidon himself rose up to defend his kingdom, but each time he rose to the surface, he had to turn away because of the searing heat.

Jove, hearing the complaints of the waters and the earth, ascended to his throne (it is here that he covers the earth with clouds, pours out rain, and sends lightning bolts). He grasped a bolt of lightning and, like a javelin, hurled it upon chariot and charioteer. The terrified horses scattered, even as the chariot itself tilted, its wheels and axles broken, and Phaëthon, like a burning torch, was sent flying through the air, plummeting toward earth, leaving a trail of smoke and flame behind him. As a comet falls from the heavens, so the boy fell, landing, at length, in the river Eridanus. The river graciously took the broken body and bathed the burnt face. The river nymphs performed the interment and carved an epitaph upon a stone. The epitaph reads:

> In This Place Lies Phaëthon,
> Who Rose in His Father's Chariot
> With a Daring beyond His Strength and Wisdom
> — And He Fell Far.

Apollo, weeping and grief-stricken, spent an entire day in mourning. For one single day, he never appeared. Clymene, however, wandered through this horrible landscape, seeking out her son's body. Eventually, she reached the river in Italy — the Eridanus — and wept when she found the tomb. His sisters joined her, weeping bitterly and singing dirge songs.[1]

The story continues on from here. We eventually find the sisters rooted in place, as they have transformed into trees. Their brother, Cygnus, wails so bitterly that his wailing turns him into a new creature entirely: the swan. Apollo eventually returns to his job, and his appearance restores to earth the life that was destroyed during the calamity.

Endnotes
1. Ovid's *Metamorphosis*, Book II, retold by the author.

Appendix D

FLOOD GEOLOGY

Recently there has been a strong current of geological study that flows toward supporting the idea of a global Deluge. Spearheaded by such organizations as Answers in Genesis, the Institute for Creation Research, and other similar groups, the movement attempts to explain modern geology through the lens of the global Flood. However, because the scope of this book is more focused on the literature aspect of the Deluge, and since there is already a vast amount of work on the subject of flood geology, I shall keep this section brief. The argument is as follows.

During floods — local *and* global — there is usually a large quantity of silt and sediment that gets stirred about in the churning waters. Anyone who has ever been through a severe flood can attest to this. Sediment typically sorts itself into various layers as it settles, so that the silt deposits at the bottom of a flood are, more or less, striated.[1] Over time, these deposits harden and become what is known as *sedimentary rock*. What most flood geologists assert is that, had there been a global Flood, the earth would be composed of layer upon layer of rock, which had formed by the sediment left behind during the Flood. Since this is precisely what we find in geology, the argument put forth *in support of* a global Flood is quite logical. These institutes also believe that the Deluge would result in the various layers of fossils found throughout the world.

A fossil is formed when a creature is rapidly buried under wet mud and other dirt. We have already discussed that wet sediment turns to rock over time. So do animals. As the creature decomposes, the skeleton is replaced by minerals, leaving behind bone-shaped rocks (or, if the creature is non-skeletal, like a fern, body-shaped impressions), known as fossils. The argument these institutes put forth is that the presence of fossils all over the earth indicates that, at some point, most — if not all — of the earth was under water. The presence of fossils on mountaintops is one compelling piece of evidence for their theory.

However, since the publication of Charles Lyell's geological theories in the mid-1800s, Louis Agassiz's discovery of the Ice Age in 1836, and the introduction of *uniformitarian geology*, modern geologists prefer to think that the processes responsible for these layers of fossils were long, slow processes, taking millions upon millions of years. One thing in particular that they noticed was that the earth — as seen when exposed in canyons — is layered. Since we cannot physically see the earth layering today, they believed that it must happen slowly, perhaps hundreds of years *per layer*. Since the earth's crust is visibly made up of hundreds of layers, and if each layer takes hundreds of years to form, then the earth must be extremely old. (At the time, the general consensus was that the earth was around 100,000 years old. This has since been expanded to approximately four billion years old.) This is, in fact, the very basis for uniformitarian geology: geological processes today have always happened at the same rate. What this interpretation does ignore, however, are catastrophic events, such as the global Deluge.

While flood geologists have compelling evidence to counteract this "uniformitarian ideology," this is still a widely debated and controversial topic among the scientific community. See the "Further Reading" section for more information.

Endnotes
1. H.A. Makse, S. Havlin, P.R. King, and H.E. Stanley, "Spontaneous Stratification in Granular Mixtures," *Nature*. Issue 386 (1997): p. 379–382.

FURTHER READING

Bright, Michael. *There Are Giants in the Sea: Monsters and Mysteries of the Depths Explored*. London: Robson Books, 1989.

Buck, William. *Ramayana*. Berkeley, CA: University of California Press, 1976.

Dundes, Alan, editor. *Sacred Narratives, Readings in the Theory of Myth*. Berkeley, CA: University of California Press, 1984.

Ellis, Richard. *Monsters of the Sea*. New York: Lyons Press, 2001.

Feldmann, Susan, editor. *African Myths and Tales*. New York: Dell, 1963.

Gaster, Theodor H. *Myth, Legend, and Custom in the Old Testament: A Comparative Study with Chapters from Sir James Frazer's Folklore in the Old Testament*. New York: Harper & Row, 1969.

Hancock, Graham. *Fingerprints of the Gods*. New York: Crown Publishers, 1995.

Hancock, Graham. *Underworld: The Mysterious Origins of Civilization*. New York: Three Rivers Press, 2003.

Hancock, Graham, and Robert Bauval. *The Message of the Sphinx: A Quest for the Hidden Legacy of Mankind*. New York: Three Rivers Press, 1996.

Homer. *The Iliad*.

Homer. *The Odyssey*.

Maggi, María Elena. *The Great Canoe: A Kariña Legend*. Translated by Elisa Amado. Toronto, ON: Groundwood/Douglas & McIntyre, 2001.

The *Mahābhārata*.

McDowell, Josh. *A Ready Defense*. Nashville, TN: T. Nelson, 1993.

Morris, Henry. *The Beginning of the World: A Scientific Study of Genesis 1–11.* Green Forest, AR: Master Books, 1991.

Oard, Mike. *Flood by Design.* Green Forest, AR: Master Books, 2008.

Ovid. *Metamorphoses.*

Ryan, William, and Walter Pitman. *Noah's Flood: The New Scientific Discoveries about the Event That Changed History.* New York: Simon & Schuster, 1998.

Stroup, Herbert. *Like a Great River: An Introduction to Hinduism.* New York: Harper & Row, 1972.

van Nooten, Barend A. *The Mahābhārata.* New York: Twayne Publishers, 1971.

Woodmorappe, John. *The Mythology of Modern Dating Methods.* El Cajon, CA: Institute for Creation Research, 1999.

Woodmorappe, John. *Noah's Ark: A Feasibility Study.* Santee, CA: Institute for Creation Research, 1996.

Woodmorappe, John. *Studies in Flood Geology.* El Cajon, CA: Institute for Creation Research, 1999.